DiGiTAL
FAMILIES

Published by Scepter Publishers, Inc.
info@scepterpublishers.org
www.scepterpublishers.org
800-322-8773
New York

Translated by Patricia Bailey Arceo
Text and cover by Rose Design

Library of Congress Cataloging-in-Publication Data

Names: Abad Domingo, Alfredo, author.
Title: Digital families : tips and guidelines for living in an online society / Alfred Domingo.
Other titles: Familias digitales. English
Description: New York : Scepter Publishers, Inc., [2016] | "This is a translation and revision of Familias digitales: claves y consejos para convivir en una sociedad en red, copyright 2015, Ediciones Palabra, S.A., Madrid, Spain [by Alfredo Abad Domingo]."
Identifiers: LCCN 2016033638 | ISBN 9781594172588 (pbk. : alk. paper)
Subjects: LCSH: Internet and families. | Internet and children. | Internet and youth. | Internet users. | Internet--Social aspects.
Classification: LCC HQ784.I58 .A2313 2016 | DDC 302.23/1--dc23
LC record available at https://lccn.loc.gov/2016033638

Digital Families PB
978-1-59417-258-8
Digital Families eBook
978-1-59417-259-5

DIGITAL FAMILIES

Tips and Guidelines for Living in an Online Society

Alfred Domingo

Scepter

Contents

Prologue

THE INTERNET HAS BECOME part of today's culture.

As a matter of course, science has become part of daily life through technical know-how.

When a new technology begins to take root, its novelty powerfully impacts how far it spreads. It tends to take root somewhat slowly, and it is expensive to use.

After some time, innovative processes are developed and the technology becomes popularized. Manufacturers can lower their prices, and the positive feedback cycle of technological implementation begins. If different areas of human activity begin to use that technology, it manages to detach itself from its scientific origins and it becomes culture. This is what has happened with Information and Communications Technologies (ICT)—in particular with the Internet.

The Internet has changed the way we carry out many activities that used to be manual and are now technological, or were once analog and are now digital. Without a doubt, the Internet has drastically changed our way of life and our culture.

A new way of life, which the internet has given us, has important implications in all aspects: physical, professional, social, economic, and moral. Therefore, we must look at new technologies from a multi-disciplinary perspective, which is what we aim to do in this book.

The Internet does not equal danger nor does it equal success. We cannot demonize technology—in whatever form—due to its novelty. Neither can we bless it for that same reason. Yet it is not hard to find people who curse technology because it is new, thus showing an irrationality of which they most likely are not even aware.

It seems that the right approach is to take an integrative attitude. Incorporating technology into our own cultural patrimony will boost our social interaction, and that will open up new opportunities to do good to others.

In communication, we pay more attention when we use more of our senses. Psychologist Edgar Dale explained this human potential in his famous Cone of Experience.[1] We learn more if we read and listen than if we just listen. Learning grows if we add visual elements, and it is enhanced even more if we apply what we learn or teach it to others.

It is surprising to see how much power a moving image has to capture a child's attention. We could say the same of a gamer's intense focus on his video game: Nothing can distract him, and he might be incapable of leaving the game even when other, more important matters call for his attention. If we are able to get control over these appetites and put them in perspective, however, we will be ready to make the most of those media and get new and better results from them.

Learning through the new technologies involves reading texts, seeing images and videos, listening to sounds, interacting with the learning platform, and relating socially with other participants. That is why it has such an irresistible capacity to grab our attention—and create addictions. Yet it also presents new challenges to learning, and it can

---

1. See *https://en.wikipedia.org/wiki/Edgar_Dale*.

improve our productivity—opportunities we should neither squander nor scorn.

The reader can approach this book on two levels: One is basic, more on the technical or utilitarian side. The other is deeper and more reflective, leading to an intellectual and moral basis for understanding this new culture.

Before handing over my manuscript to the printers, I incorporated the changes suggested by professionals in the fields of education, family counseling, psychology, and also by various experts who examined this book from the point of view of their own professions, and for whose help I am grateful: Alberto, Fernando, Mamen, Javier, Aida, and others who prefer to remain unnamed but who helped me a great deal, especially Tomás T., who took care of an in-depth first revision. And, as it is now a custom in my books, I dedicate these words to my parents, from whom I have received everything.

1

"MAYBE THIS ISN'T MY THING"

YOU MIGHT THINK THAT TECHNOLOGY is "not your thing." Perhaps you are not a total technophobe, but you don't consider yourself a technophile either. Or maybe the Internet's services are somehow insignificant to your daily life. If this describes the way you think, this book is not only a good fit for you—you also need it. Why? Because you have not yet realized that the Internet has become culture in our midst, and we cannot work in society from a position of cultural uprootedness. If you live in this society, the Internet affects you, whether you like it or not. That is to say, it is "your thing."

> The Internet has become part of the cultural substrate in which all of society's individuals are rooted.

Many people are not aware of the importance of technology or the Internet in their own daily lives. Technology is just one more element of their lives, and in some cases, a structural element of other activities. They are those who have not had to put forth any effort to get it, because they have always experienced it. These

1

are the so-called "digital natives." In our society, almost all teenagers, and particularly all children, are digital natives. They have no trouble programming the television remote control, they are familiar with and can install applications on smartphones, and they play games online with others—friends or strangers—through their tablets.

Then there are the people who use technology with ease, but who have known other times; that is, they have known other ways of doing things or relating to others. These are the "digital immigrants." They know how to use technology and may even have serious addictions to it, but they know from experience that there are more possibilities than merely technological ones.

Finally, there are those—ever fewer—who have no connection to technology because technological processes are beyond their reach (digital illiterates) or because they think the path that leads to their life's destiny has nothing to do with technology. This group includes some older people with cognitive or relational difficulties, as well as people who have not had the chance to encounter technology in an enriching way.

CHARACTERISTICS OF THE TECHNOLOGICAL PHENOTYPES

Before listing each group's traits, we must understand why it's important to study this in the first place. The reason is simple: We should know how people in each of the groups behave in order to argue more effectively about the risks and potential of technology.

Except for extreme cases, nobody fits perfectly or exclusively into the above categories. Most of us usually have

Digital Natives	Digital Immigrants	Digital Illiterates
Multitask and use multimedia.	Multitask but take it for granted.	Work on one task at a time.
Only learn through graphic documents: image, video, 3D. Openly immersed in electronic devices.	Access digital media but end up printing what they read. Use electronic devices but are not immersed in them.	Obtain knowledge from printed media only. Do not use electronic devices.
Use all available smartphone services.	Use cell phones and some simple applications.	Sometimes use cell phones, but only to make calls.
Share information on social networks but never save the information. Social networks are their natural relationship and communications media.	Save information that interests them, and if they share it, they do so through email. Use social networks sporadically.	Need others to get access to digital content. Cannot communicate through social networks.
Make decisions instantly, including important ones.	Thoughtful and generally slow to make decisions.	Slow and detailed in their activities.
Play electronically with all kinds of devices. Play is seen as a fundamental activity.	See electronic games as just another activity, not a particularly important one.	See video games as irrelevant to their lives.
Look and *Google* are synonymous.	Use Wikipedia articles or go directly to a website for reliable information.	Rely on books when searching for information.

Continued

Continued

Digital Natives	Digital Immigrants	Digital Illiterates
Places little importance on digital or electronic updates because they are already a natural part of their usual activity.	Fear new software versions or the replacement of electronic devices, but resign themselves to them.	Technological innovation does not interest them at all.
Handle change with ease.	See changes as obstacles and must make an effort to overcome them.	See change as more than an obstacle; it is a chasm they might not be able to cross.

some elements of all three. However, there is always one that is dominant.

> Reflect on your own situation and try to classify yourself or the people around you into one of these three groups. This information will later help you to discover concrete solutions to possible problems that might arise in each model, or to come up with strategies for improvement.

There is also a heterogeneous group of high-risk cases among people who love technology deeply and could not survive without it (technophiles) and also among those who hate or reject any technological change in their lives (technophobes). These two positions are deeply irrational. The people in either of these stances are more at risk for manipulation, deceit, and even tragedy, because they exclude themselves socially, becoming misfits or ending up *digitally marginalized.*

Another term some have begun to use lately is "digital orphans," referring to children who use technology without the help and guidance of their parents. This occurs when either their parents cannot provide the help (perhaps they are digital illiterates) or because, as digital immigrants or natives, they do not consider it important or do not have time for it.

FORMATION IS THE TREASURE CHEST OF SUCCESS

Formation is another word for *education*. Formation leads us to know the solid and true foundations on which to build our way of living and behaving. A person with formation is not immovable, but instead changes his position when new circumstances call for it. And such a person applies the necessary means to change himself or transform the reality around him according to what he thinks he must do.

THE WELL-FORMED PERSON

- Knows himself (the truth of who he is).
- Knows reality (the truth of what surrounds him).
- Knows how he should relate to reality (the truth of his sociability).
- Knows the ways to get from where he is to where he wants to be (the truth of his transformative capacity).
- Decides, through reflection, which of those ways is the most appropriate and decides to pursue it (prudence).
- Is equipped (thanks to the human virtues) with the ability to overcome the difficulties that crop up in the path freely chosen.

This complex process depends entirely on freedom; without which it cannot happen or would be hampered.

A well-equipped reader, such as one who dares to read this book, will realize that one's formation shapes one's way of thinking and acting according to one's being, one's personal dignity.

> F ormation is a process of change that perfects us.

There are those who think the entire formative process is manipulative, but this is not the case. Formation and manipulation (i.e., deformation) both invite us to change, but formation does it by perfecting what we are (it is anthropologically coherent), while manipulation corrupts us as persons and dehumanizes us.

At this point, we can now begin to reflect independently on the matter at hand. The cell phone, the tablet, and the Internet open up new possibilities that we absolutely cannot dismiss. But does my personal growth depend only on doing everything that it is possible for me to do? We have already seen that the answer is no—we have to take into account who we are, how we are, where we want to go, and then choose the right means. We cannot do anything at any price. Our choices should lead to our own betterment as people, and thus we can conclude that not everything new is good, nor is everything old necessarily bad; not everything new is useful, nor is everything old outdated. And not everything that can be done should be done.

Therefore, if we want technology to become part of our lives in a human and reasonable way, we have to use our freedom to do *what we must* because *it is good to do it,* which is very different from doing something because we have the opportunity to do it.

But personal freedom is challenging, because using it requires making an effort to *know what we should do* (acquire formation) and then *strive to do it* (and this requires human virtues).

When educating children or teenagers, we realize they need an apprenticeship in order to use the Internet well. Why? Because their formative process is not yet finished. That is why parents and educators, who are responsible for their formation, should help them to moderate their activity with some complementary norms or rules of the game.

And are adults problem-free? Adults shouldn't use the Internet indiscriminately either. Adults typically have had more formation, which helps them use their freedom better. But they can also misuse their freedom, no matter how old they are. So what we say here for minors also applies to adults, with some differences.

Smoking or drinking alcohol harms a child's health. It also harms an adult's health. But while the law prohibits the selling of tobacco or alcoholic drinks to minors, it doesn't apply to adults. Is it odd that the law penalizes a harmful thing in some cases but not in others?

This example can help us understand that we should not get stuck on whether something *can or cannot be done* from a legal standpoint, but rather we should focus on *whether it should or should not be done*—whether it is good or bad from a moral standpoint.

Morality is not a collection of prohibitions and capricious orders; it is a guide that takes our nature and personal dignity into account as it points us toward the good, toward what perfects us and leads us to happiness. The fact that the law allows adults to buy alcohol does not make it good for adults to consume as much alcohol as they please. Not everything that is legal is moral, just as not everything that is immoral is illegal.

Pornography on the Internet does great damage to minors, and parents would do well to block their children's access to pages that show it. But this measure is ineffective if parents are not able to explain to their children *why* looking at pornography on their cell phone is damaging to them and why they should not do it. It is not enough for parents to erect domestic "legal" barriers. They have to form their children so their children know what they should do, what is good and why, what is bad and why, and then decide freely and personally to do what is good because they *want* to do it. Once more, it becomes clear that there is no efficacy without formation.

REMEMBER:

1. The Internet has become part of our culture, so we cannot uproot ourselves from it and live on the margins.
2. Any kind of extreme or irrational attitude toward the technological world is deeply damaging.
3. Only through formation in the new technologies can we avoid being manipulated.

2

———— · ————

ON THEIR SCREENS:
THE NEW TECHNOLOGIES

WHEN WE TALK ABOUT the new technologies, what technologies are we referring to? Which of them are the new ones?

The concept of *new technologies* is as broad as it is muddled. Any innovative technology is automatically labeled as a "new technology." Yet the adjective *new* does not refer to newness in a chronological sense, but rather in terms of its impact on human activity or culture.

Today there are new technologies related to biology or biochemistry (genetic advances, stem cell research), new materials physicists are studying (grapheme, superconductors), and technologies related to information and communication. We are interested in the latter, and we will refer to them throughout this book as TIC (Technologies of Information and Communication) or IT (Information Technologies).

These technologies make up our global communications landscape, which affects all of us and crosscuts all human activity. We have to get used to living on these frontiers. It requires an adaptation process (except for those digital natives) and the creation of a new culture that values and reformulates the novelties, putting them at the service of humanity. That is, without realizing it, we have become extras in a new movie in which science fiction becomes palpable reality.

WHO ARE THE ACTORS—THE CAST—OF THIS STORY?

In the family setting, *the main stars are the parents.* Even when the issue is a minor's access to the Internet or a video game, the parents are still—and now more than ever—the protagonists. And I do not simply mean that they have to take responsibility a minor cannot completely take on— parents have to be true protagonists, active agents, sources of initiatives, evaluators of measures, and catalysts of their children's activities.

In a school setting, *the teachers and educational system* are responsible for what happens in the classroom and for the type of formation provided there. But the leading stars are still the parents, because they are the ones who decide what type of education to give their children. Thus, while the teachers and schools are necessary for the movie, they are only supporting actors.

There are also extras in the movie. The TICs are used as a service, and so there are many other *agents providing services* who have a great deal of influence both on the information consumed and the way in which it is consumed, making up a backdrop that is not necessarily innocuous. It is true that they are not protagonists, but the script offers them many nuances and possibilities, because they are the channels through which the plot unfolds.

Some of these agents who provide services—our extras— are telephone and Internet operators, websites and blogs, virtual stores, video game sites, social networks, electronic messaging sites, manufacturers of electronic devices (telephones, tablets, computers, and gadgets in general).

What about the minors? What role do they play? For me, it is clear: They are *spectators*. But they are not passive spectators. In fact, they are very active and deeply receptive of everything that happens on the screen with which they interact. They undergo influences and pressures in various areas, both external and internal. From the outside, they are affected by all the actors we mentioned before: Their parents and teachers tell them what to do, the schools make demands on them, the service providers tell them what they should consume and how. But their interior disposition also plays a role, since their actions depend on their level of formation, their character, their human virtues, and whether they trust the adults in case they find themselves facing a problem.

Initially, we might think that minors are the protagonists in our story, but this is not the case. They are rather the receivers of others' activity. Nevertheless, a minor can also become an actor, such as when he or she relates actively to other people through social networks. Minors can be bullied, but they can also be the bullies. That is why minors must be given limits, but they should be understandable and reasonable limits—limits that can be discussed (in an appropriate way, according to the minors' age) and that are neither so harsh nor so light that they end up nonexistent in practice.

> How do we achieve this? As always, the parents and teachers need formation, as do the minors. The key to the reasonable consumption of technology is in the free exercise of prudence.

THE PROPS: THE SPECIFIC ASPECTS OF EVERY TYPE OF MEDIA

The agents—our actors—exercise their role through the different technologies and the devices and services they use to consume them. In our analogy, these media are the *movie props*. Every communications media, every technology, every service has its own idiosyncrasies we should be aware of; we should know what advantages they offer and what risks we take on when we decide to use them. We will dedicate the following chapters to those media.

REMEMBER:

1. Parents are the true protagonists, active agents, sources of initiatives, evaluators of media, and catalysts of their children's activities.
2. The minor receives the activity of the others.
3. We must be familiar with all forms of media to which all agents in the communications world can be exposed.

3

VIDEO GAMES AND GAMIFICATION

VIDEO AND COMPUTER GAMES INSPIRE great passion in the younger generation. Of course, since those first generations of video game players have been adults for some time, we now have families where both children and their parents play, although not always the same games. Keep this in mind as you read the paragraphs that follow.

Video games were first conceived for playing on television. Electronic games were executed through primitive consoles that sent a signal to the television. Players interacted with the electronic game through a button or joystick on the console. At that stage video games were merely entertainment. Parents of a certain age—and some grandparents, too—have this concept of video games. However, video games are no longer like that today.

Today's video games have come a long way from their origins a few decades ago . . .

The next generation of video games were computer programs that could be played on personal computers, which multiplied their possibilities enormously, as well as their risks: wasted time, addiction, piracy, and so on. The first personal consoles also appeared, making it possible for people to play anytime and anyplace. A great moment for video games appeared when people began to talk about using video games as an educational tool.

Since games have a great capacity for emulation, they can be used as an instrument for professional training. The context in which we interact with a game allows for the creation of a virtual or fictional reality—one that goes beyond mere entertainment and can stimulate or exploit nonrational elements, or at least unconscious ones.

ONLINE GAMING

Video games next moved to the Internet and can now be played anywhere; a personal computer and video console are no longer necessary. They can be played on one's cell phone, tablet, or any modern gadget; there's no need to install the video game on these devices, since it is hosted on the Web, in the cloud. This feature also enables the interaction of multiple users with the same game, so the video game can "virtualize" human relations. This increases the possibilities for communication, but also the risks.

> The gaming industry is full of commercial interests.

In this panorama, it is clear that the gaming industry is not neutral; on the contrary, it is full of commercial interests. In fact, in computer science, the gaming sector is more profitable than all the rest combined. This alone is enough to realize that it is irresponsible to give a minor access to a video game without first having taken some prudent measures. Video consoles are now as powerful as, or even more powerful than, desktop computers and they are connected to the Internet.

Video games are still forms of entertainment, but they are more than that.

They are also a means for training, emulation, education, relaxation, skills acquisition, and more. On the other hand, they can also be a waste of time, a cause of lack of attention, pornographic, violent, bullying, and identity replacement. Everything is on the Web, accessed from any device, with full virtual connection to any other player in anyplace and at anytime.

> Gaming without any control leads to gaming addictions and causes situations of social isolation in which virtual reality takes on a disproportionate role.

Just as it seems natural for us to set a television schedule or choose programs for the whole family to watch, it should also be natural to propose a schedule, choose the video games, and let various members of the family participate. In fact, most of today's video consoles allow for multiple players, which allows the fictitious relationship between players to become a relationship that is real, close, and based on affection.

> On the other hand, when parents prohibit a child from watching television, playing a specific video game, or—on another level—when a counselor advises the parents to reduce their children's consumption, it is not a good idea to propose this initiative out of the blue. *It is useless to ban a video game if there is no*

> *specific alternative to take its place.* It is not enough to say, "Don't do this." Rather, we have to say, "Instead of that, do this other thing." We can reduce television time by substituting family games, replace single-player video games with multi-player games involving other family members, and so on.

Electronic betting and electronic gambling deserve special mention. The convenience of playing from home and doing it almost anonymously can lead more easily to a gambling addiction and an excessive exposure to online fraud. In the best of cases, it will lead to a serious waste of time.

THE GAMIFICATION OF EDUCATION

Recently, some educators began talking about *gamification*, which is a new pedagogical approach that brings gaming techniques into nongaming fields. This involves teaching methods that stimulate the student with the achievement of goals and objectives, turning the learning process into a digital scoreboard and making the learning process a game. Electronic gaming does not work for everyone, however. In fact, it reveals a big difference between the majority of children who like gaming and who would spend all their free time on it if they could and those who are somewhat clumsy at it and usually dislike it.

> Gaming can be a good way to learn, but . . . there is a but. Gaming causes a high level of stimulus in the gamer, who plays in a hyper-motivated state. Learning does take place in that almost-permanent state of hyper-motivation. But if we only use gaming as a

teaching tool, what will happen in real life when that child has to perform tasks that are not particularly motivating, or are downright boring? He will not be able to make that effort if he has not sufficiently developed the virtue of fortitude.

Thus, while gamification in education can be a viable teaching tool (although not necessarily the most effective one), it should not dominate the entire learning process. It should instead serve as a complement. Many of the learning applications for digital tablets, especially for children, offer solutions based on gratification and can greatly enhance learning. However, they can also undermine the learning process if children are not also taught personal virtues—not just values, but actual virtues that internalize the value in the specific and unique person.

> We have to combine gamification with other approaches that foster personal virtues.

It is a good idea to use educational video games at home and in school. There are many of them, and they strengthen kids' skills, increasing their desire to learn and fostering a love of reading. However, before buying them, it is important to obtain enough information about the video game, and then make sure that it is doing what it is supposed to do for the child.

I do not want to criminalize *role-playing games*, because they are not necessarily damaging by virtue of using role playing, but I do think some risks should be pointed out. In these games, the player has to assume a specific psychological or operational profile that is not his own. If the child is able to separate reality from fiction, this is fine. But if this is not the case and the child spends a lot of time playing, this activity can become a serious problem for the child, who might put so much into the role that he can begin to suffer personality confusion and require the help of a specialist in psychology or psychiatry.

When it comes to video games, there is a whole range of possibilities. There are wonderful things, and there are horrible things, more horrible than you think. When you decide to buy a video game, please research it first. Later we will offer some tips on how to do so.

Finally, we have to consider another device: the smart TV, which lets us enjoy the programming of a conventional television with the added value of an Internet connection that allows us to interact through social networks. With the smart TV, the television is no longer just a passive device; it becomes a new relational element. The doors to interactive television are opened, again with many possibilities but also risks.

THE CLASSIFICATION OF VIDEO GAMES

In most countries, commercial video games are subjected to a classification that codifies the type of game and the recommended ages. The most frequent classification system in the United States, Canada, and Mexico is established by the Entertainment Software Rating Board (ESRB). The ESRB is a self-regulatory organization that assigns age and content ratings, enforces industry-adopted advertising guidelines, and ensures responsible online privacy principles for computer and video games. The ratings are assigned based on a game's content, similar to the motion picture rating systems used in many countries. The

ESRB uses a combination of six age-based levels designed to help consumers determine a game's content and suitability. The ESRB also maintains a code of ethics for the advertising and promotion of video games. The ESRB is also a member of the International Age Rating Coalition.[1] Participation in the rating system by game manufacturers is voluntary but almost all video games sold by retailers or downloaded to a game system in Canada or the United States are rated by the ESRB. In fact, major retailers only stock and sell games with an ESRB rating.

The ESBR classification has three parts: categories that designate the level of maturity intended to play the game, the content of the game that substantiates the classification, and the interaction component—whether the game involves contact with others on the web and what information is shared during that interaction.

The ESRB classification guidelines are as follows:

 Early childhood: Content is intended for young children.

 Everyone: Content is generally suitable for all ages. May contain minimal cartoon, fantasy or mild violence and/or infrequent use of mild language.

 Everyone 10+: Content is generally suitable for ages 10 and up. May contain more cartoon, fantasy or mild violence, mild language and/or minimal suggestive themes.

---

1. From Wikipedia, The Entertainment Software Rating Board, *en.wikipedia. org/wiki/Entertainment_Software Rating_Board.*

Teen: Content is generally suitable for ages 13 and up. May contain violence, suggestive themes, crude humor, minimal blood, simulated gambling and/or infrequent use of strong language.

 Mature: Content is generally suitable for ages 17 and up. May contain intense violence, blood and gore, sexual content and/or strong language.

 Adults only: Content suitable only for adults ages 18 and up. May include prolonged scenes of intense violence, graphic sexual content and/or gambling with real currency.

 Rating pending: Not yet assigned a final ESRB rating. Appears only in advertising, marketing and promotional materials related to a "boxed" video game that is expected to carry an ESRB rating, and should be replaced by a game's rating once it has been assigned.[2]

The ESRB content descriptors are

- Alcohol Reference—Reference to and/or images of alcoholic beverages
- Animated Blood—Discolored and/or unrealistic depictions of blood
- Blood—Depictions of blood
- Blood and Gore—Depictions of blood or the mutilation of body parts

---

2. From *http://www.esrb.org/ratings/ratings_guide.aspx.*

- Cartoon Violence—Violent actions involving cartoon-like situations and characters. May include violence where a character is unharmed after the action has been inflicted
- Comic Mischief—Depictions or dialogue involving slapstick or suggestive humor
- Crude Humor—Depictions or dialogue involving vulgar antics, including "bathroom" humor
- Drug Reference—Reference to and/or images of illegal drugs
- Fantasy Violence—Violent actions of a fantasy nature, involving human or non-human characters in situations easily distinguishable from real life
- Intense Violence—Graphic and realistic-looking depictions of physical conflict. May involve extreme and/or realistic blood, gore, weapons and depictions of human injury and death
- Language—Mild to moderate use of profanity
- Lyrics—Mild references to profanity, sexuality, violence, alcohol or drug use in music
- Mature Humor—Depictions or dialogue involving "adult" humor, including sexual references
- Nudity—Graphic or prolonged depictions of nudity
- Partial Nudity—Brief and/or mild depictions of nudity
- Real Gambling—Player can gamble, including betting or wagering real cash or currency
- Sexual Content—Non-explicit depictions of sexual behavior, possibly including partial nudity
- Sexual Themes—References to sex or sexuality
- Sexual Violence—Depictions of rape or other violent sexual acts

- Simulated Gambling—Player can gamble without betting or wagering real cash or currency
- Strong Language—Explicit and/or frequent use of profanity
- Strong Lyrics—Explicit and/or frequent references to profanity, sex, violence, alcohol or drug use in music
- Strong Sexual Content—Explicit and/or frequent depictions of sexual behavior, possibly including nudity
- Suggestive Themes—Mild provocative references or materials
- Tobacco Reference—Reference to and/or images of tobacco products
- Use of Alcohol—The consumption of alcoholic beverages
- Use of Drugs—The consumption or use of illegal drugs
- Use of Tobacco—The consumption of tobacco products
- Violence—Scenes involving aggressive conflict. May contain bloodless dismemberment
- Violent References—References to violent acts[3]

Each commercial product classified through ESRB is required to include identification labels. "Packaged or boxed games display an ESRB Rating Category on the front of the box and Content Descriptors on the back. Digitally delivered games and apps, such as those that are downloaded directly to a game system or mobile device, present the ESRB rating prior to download."[4]

---

3. Ibid.
4. From *http://www.esrb.org/ratings/faq.aspx#10*.

REMEMBER:

1. Since gaming allows for a high degree of emulation, it can be used as a tool for professional training.
2. In the computer industry, video games bring in more profits than all of the other sectors together.
3. Just as it seems natural to us to set a television schedule and choose programs that can be watched as a family, it is also natural to choose the video games, propose a schedule, and have various members of the family participate.
4. Gamification in pedagogy runs the risk of encouraging the child to make an effort only when it is attractive and profitable for him, ignoring more tedious but important tasks.

4

MOBILE DEVICES

IN THIS CHAPTER, WE WILL DISCUSS smartphones and digital tablets—that is, electronic devices that connect us to communication networks and allow users to interact with the services offered on these networks through touch screens or similar gadgets.

The first specific characteristic of these devices is that they allow for a large variety of possibilities for users to connect to their environment, which makes them extraordinarily versatile. In addition, since they are lightweight devices and not subjected to the slavery of cables, they allow users to move around. They can be used anywhere and anytime, "here and now."

The functionality of mobile devices increases prodigiously with the installation of a range of applications (apps, in technical jargon), which are downloaded from repositories or virtual stores associated with the manufacturers of the devices or software developers. Many apps cost something, but most are free. In any case, the price of an app usually tends to be quite low. The manufacturers of these paid apps assume that, since there will be many sales, they will reap profits on the large scale of the business. The makers of free apps make a profit through advertising or by associating the apps to other payment services.

The important thing to bear in mind is that there are good apps and not-so-good apps. Some of them involve going through a payment process and inputting credit card information, which then remains registered in some depository in the device that executes the purchase—posing an added risk.

On the other hand, we have to consider security issues. Eugene Kaspersky, the founder of the well-known security company, warned that cyber warfare could destroy the world as we know it.[1] A recent study from the Spanish National Institute of Communication Technologies (INTECO) confirmed that three out of every ten unauthorized software downloads in Spain have a virus.[2]

The apps are not completely innocent, either. They can seem like simple electronic windows giving us a peek into the digital world, but they are much more than that. Most of the apps invite users to establish a relationship with some remote service. In the traditional applications, the information with which they operate is in the same device that executes the application. For example, if you write a text with a word processor, the information is stored in the same place where that document is processed. However, what usually happens with apps is that, although they are run on a cell phone or on a tablet, the data does not necessarily

1. Robert Richardson, "Cyber Warfare Apocalypse—Experts Warn End of the World as We Know It Scenario Might Be Close," *http://offgridsurvival. com/cyber-teotwawki/*.

2. *Study on the Security Risks Arising from Unauthorized Use Software,* Spanish National Institute of Communication Technologies, INTECO, May 2012, p. 7.

stay on the phone or in the tablet, but in the "cloud," that is, in a storage service on the other side of the Internet. Therefore, without the Internet there is no service, and the app would be useless. This means that the apps—we are speaking generically here—are runways to the Internet with a certain added value. The app manufacturer leads us by the information that he cares about and in the amount he decides to give. As we can imagine, this has big advantages, since many apps are educational, but it also has some drawbacks. Be that as it may, the mobility of electronic devices means that

- *They can be used anytime*, which means they blur the distinction of when one should and should not use a device.
- *They can be used anywhere,* as long as there is connection coverage, which means that they can be used in any place, or situation.
- *They can create dependencies* on one or various service providers, such as the telephone company, the Internet provider, or the software developer, which leads to consumer weakness.

The use of mobile devices has changed our relationships with our workplaces and schools. In a process known as "consumerization," employees of businesses and students in educational centers now want information readily available on their tablets or smartphones. Employees, clients, and students expect access at anytime and anywhere on their low-cost mobile devices. Also, a phenomenon called BYOD (Bring Your Own Device) allows consumers to access everything a company or supplier offers on their mobile device. This basically encourages people to focus on consuming above all else. Without additional prudential measures, this readily available information on an always available device amounts to turning on the television and passively expecting to be entertained.

> Since the main characteristic of mobile devices is their portability—that's precisely why they are mobile—it's important to show courtesy to others when out and about. It is very unpleasant to be talking to someone and suffer constant interruptions because he or she answers calls every few minutes. Sometimes this can't be helped, but on most occasions the calls, texts, or emails can wait. Our use of the new technologies should not eclipse good manners, common courtesy, or our respect for others. If you think this advice doesn't apply to you, ask a few people: Perhaps you will be surprised.

COMPULSIVE BEHAVIOR AND BLACKBERRY THUMB

The overuse of mobile devices can lead to obsessive behaviors. These odd behaviors, which limit or weaken the freedom to act, are what psychologists call "compulsions." When people base their activity on reason, they are more likely to protect themselves from potential compulsions because they become masters of their own behavior.

Compulsion is a behavior characterized by a lack of freedom to act purposefully.

Those who dedicate themselves to studying the effects of technology have observed a compulsive phenomenon that is actually very alarming. Many adolescents and even adults exhibit a compulsive urge to be constantly connected, sending messages and receiving communications. Much of the time, most of it has no value and no purpose. And if, by some chance, they lose their connection, they also lose their composure and even their appetite. These individuals appear to have an intense social network, but in reality there is no exchange of intimacy or values, no real relationships but merely an activity toward which their digital compulsion is constantly pushing them.

This phenomenon has been on the rise with the proliferation of mobile devices, as psychologists and educational psychologists are well aware. New forms of osteoarthritis have resulted from repetitive typing, known as "Blackberry Thumb"[3] and "cell phone elbow" (similar to tennis elbow but without the racket, and instead of the elbow being affected, it's the thumb).[4]

Along the same lines, think back to the era when the Sony Walkman first appeared, followed by MP3 players. Every adolescent with one of these music-playing devices walked around wearing headphones all the time. It was hard to talk to them because their headphones kept them almost totally isolated. Now the same thing is happening with the demanding and constant attention to the cell phone, social media, email, and text messages.

---

3. Daniel J. DeNoon, "Blackberry Thumb: Real Illness or Just Dumb?," 2005, *http://www.webmd.com/arthritis/news/20050126/blackberry-thumb-real-illness-just-dumb*.

4. Katherine Harmon, "Is There Such a Thing as 'Cell Phone Elbow'?," June 4, 2009, *http://www.scientificamerican.com/article/what-is-cell-phone-elbow/*.

It is not unusual today to find kids in school sending each other text messages during recess, even though they might be sitting together on the same bench. The important thing in this case is not what they have to say, but the medium they use to communicate. This is one more example of why Marshall McLuhan, the promoter of information highways, says: "The medium is the message" and believes we are living in an "electronic global village."[5] We end up confusing *content* and *continent*, something very typical of postmodern deconstruction. Little by little, technology has turned education into a *commodity* that is more *industry* than *craftsmanship*.

CELL PHONES: PROBLEM OR SOLUTION?

The youth especially take a tremendous interest in electronic messaging. In fact, text messaging has far outstripped the appeal of voice calls.

> Let's suppose that your son begins his study time. Perhaps it has not been easy for him to achieve it, but he has overcome the initial barrier and has gotten down to work. To measure the time he is dedicating to his studies, he has his cell phone on top of his desk, using it as a clock. Sometimes he gets a message, which he answers if it is something important, and then he continues studying. He may receive a few phone calls from classmates who ask him a question or check in with him about possible plans. To this we can add the interruptions from incoming texts. Every time

5. James C. Morrison Jr., "Marshall McLuhan: No Prophet without Honor," December 2, 1999, *http://www.mit.edu/~saleem/ivory/ch2.htm.*

someone uses the app to send a group message, his phone makes a sound or vibrates, which distracts him. If his group is made up of twenty people—his closest friends—and each of them writes one message per hour to the group, every one of them will get twenty messages per hour, amounting to an interruption every three minutes.

Is it possible for a person to study like that? It's not that your son doesn't want to study; he simply can't. His work conditions make it impossible.

We can change his room but it is useless, because the cell phone can go with him. We can change his study schedule, but that is also useless, because cell phones are independent of time. And group messaging apps—services that are often free—result, most of the time, in messages that are not important. Since the cost is the same to send a message to one person or to a group of people, users frequently choose to send messages to a long list of contacts. Sending messages is not more expensive when there are more recipients, but the amount of time lost in reading and answering unimportant messages does come with a cost. In fact, as the size of the group increases, the more likely that the recipients will receive messages that are unimportant, and so more time misspent.

Do you know how many text messages your son or daughter sends per day, and to whom? Do you know what online groups they belong to? Do you know how many members those groups have? Do these questions help you evaluate the enormous amount of work that a minor—or an adult, for that matter— must do to respond to all these competing claims on his attention? And we have not even touched on the messages received through social media networks, which we will talk about later.

Some parents are fooled into thinking that the best way to keep an eye on their children is to give them a mobile phone. They think naively that they can call their children at any time or, if they need help, their children will be able to call them. It is true that you can call your child and she can call you, but that does not mean that you are keeping an eye on her. When you call someone on the cell phone, do you know where they are? If you ask, they will tell you—if they want to. And if they choose to, they can also lie. Children do not lie when there is no need to. So, is this really keeping an eye on your kids? Not quite.

If a minor has problems, a cell phone is not necessarily a solution. It is similar to a weapon in their hands: Cell phones open the doors to an abundance of possibilities and a child can use it for good or bad.

Additionally, almost all cell phones today have video cameras that can sometimes be used indiscriminately. If we do not train kids how to use the video camera appropriately, they might commit a crime, even without realizing it. They can also be spied on from the other side of the Internet and may even be stalked. We will cover this problem more in depth later.

HOW MANY APPS SHOULD THEY HAVE?

Another aspect we have to keep an eye on is our kids' access to an app developer's virtual store. Ideally the installation of a new app should be done through the corresponding installation tool, which puts the user in contact with a virtual store (Apple Store for Apple devices, Google Play for those based on Android, and so on).

Many apps are free, but others are not. This means that one must provide identification to the store, as well as a credit card number or other payment mechanism accepted by the virtual store. This is risky for two reasons:

- The provider captures the credit card number, which is very sensitive information.

- The data remains on file, and if the mobile device (smartphone or tablet) has not been closed appropriately, a minor may be able to buy new products at the store. His parents will not find out until they get the credit card bill. In addition, minors will be able to consume not only apps, but also music, books, and other paid services, such as appointments, contacts, and even pornography (normally not on official sites, but definitely on alternative repositories).

Thus, one important recommendation is for the parent to install any necessary apps on their child's cell phone. Afterward the installation process should be protected insofar as it is possible so that no uncontrolled apps can enter in later. The capacity to do so depends on the type of device.

Installing apps is less risky if it is only done from the official repositories, which better guarantee that the apps that will be downloaded and installed are clean of viruses or other malwares, such as spy programs or undercover advertising. We will discuss this problem at greater length when we talk about Web services.

THE NEW POSSIBILITIES OF MOBILE DEVICES

Digital tablets are now a widespread and fundamental part of the educational scenario. Tablets open up a whole universe of new opportunities that we should not dismiss, since they are very useful. Many apps allow students to access an extensive educational curriculum. The teaching underneath these apps allows for a very specific personalization of the educational plan and timetable, which makes these apps not only versatile, but also extraordinarily suitable for reinforcing conceptual and operational learning.

> The moderate use of digital tablets in the educational environment can bring great benefits to students.

One area where tablets are essential is serving people with some handicap. A tablet can make up for a handicap and become part of an adapted learning process. For example, a child with dyslexia can improve substantially if he is given a plan based on an app designed to treat that kind of problem. If the minor is slow in mathematics, he can utilize apps to study each of the topics where he has underperformed.

Tablets and digital readers have special relevance when it comes to fostering reading. This electronic activity should be encouraged: Reading is the process by which we install new software in our mind. Digital readers effectively promote this process and can be carried around more easily than printed books. In addition, digital books are cheaper, so reading becomes more affordable. A digital reader is always a good gift for a child or an adult, since it does not put any barriers to reading. As a mobile device, it also helps people to better use their time, since it can be read anywhere. Therefore, these new media are very useful tools to increase educational performance in many areas.

> Nevertheless, let us ask ourselves some questions: Who can assure me that when my child is working with the tablet, he is using the approved app? Could he be receiving text messages that are distracting him at the same time that he is working on his grammar app? If he is writing a report, can I disable the copy/paste function to make sure his content is original? When he writes, is his spelling correct, or does he hand over that responsibility to the word processor without being aware of the mistakes he is making? If he has to look up a word that appears in his reading and he uses the Internet, will he get distracted with a navigation session that starts with that word and ends up somewhere else? Meanwhile, time is marching on.

When learning is closely driven by an application, the child may become so accustomed to relating learning to technology that he will be unable to learn when technology is missing. Once again the key to solving this problem is *moderation*—reasonably imposed by the teacher in order to help the minor build sound criteria.

If your child's school uses technology for learning, you should make sure that there is a specific plan for using such media, with defined objectives that can be evaluated, and also with the right amount of moderation. This is necessary because first, every excess is bad; and second, because the results of didactic experiments with minors will last a lifetime, whether they are good or bad. No one wants to experiment with his own children, even less when others take over that right. I am not saying we should anchor ourselves in the past, because any opportunity to learn is good, whether it comes through an electronic app or through the empathy generated in a masterfully prepared class.

> But how are you going to make sure your child does not install apps that are not good for him or simply distract him? What can you do if you see that his cell phone has apps he never uses or are counterproductive? Teach by your example, and then you will have the courage and moral authority to propose and enforce rules that will bear fruit over time.

LAPTOP COMPUTERS

Although they are less comfortable for transport, laptop computers are also mobile devices. They are widely used for creating documents or executing specific production tasks, and they also serve as a support for many electronic games. Some tasks such as navigation, digital reading, or social networking now are more frequently performed on tablets. However, laptops have some specific and relevant elements for us to consider.

First they can store much more information than a cell phone or a tablet, since they have a massive storage space of their own (for example, a hard drive). This means users can save information (programs, documents, photographs, videos) that they may never use or they may misuse.

Many of the apps that are installed on laptops or desk computers have a cost and are subject to copyrights.

Whether a particular computer application is fairly priced or not, it is morally right to respect the copyrights.

If we have to pay a few dollars for a mobile app, perhaps we do not mind very much, but if we have to pay one hundred times more for a desktop application, we might think twice about it. And we might fall for the temptation to get a pirated version because it's readily available! When we get to this point, welcome to the risk zone!

> When considering an app, ask yourself these questions: Do I need this app on my computer? Will I really use it? Also, if you do not want to pay for the apps or can't afford them, explore the world of free software. There are many good apps that are free and viable alternatives to proprietary or paid software.

In addition to the moral objection, using pirated software entails risks. Downloading pirated software can let in malware that can cause serious problems: virus, spies, video camera activations, the theft of personal data, spamming all our contacts, the loss of data, and so on. Pirated software comes with a tremendous cost.

DIGITAL DIOGENES SYNDROME

Diogenes syndrome is a behavioral disorder characterized by *voluntary social isolation*, which results in being reclusive and abandoning proper hygiene.

Those who suffer from this syndrome can accumulate large quantities of trash and waste in their homes, living in conditions that verge on extreme poverty (although in some cases they are people with high purchasing power). This syndrome was named for Diogenes of Sinope, also known as the Cynic, who heralded an austere lifestyle and renounced all kinds of comforts.[6]

Today the "Digital Diogenes Syndrome"[7] refers to a psychological problem that leads people to save any music, video, or program that they find on the Internet. Most of this information is kept "just in case" or "to read later" or "for when I get bored." So much information is accumulated that the computer's hard drive runs out of space and the user has to get an external storage device.

Recently, the study *Digital Universe,* written by International Data Corporation (IDC) and sponsored by EMC, revealed that in spite of the uncontrolled growth of information stored on digital devices, only 0.5 percent of it is really analyzed. That is, 99.5 percent of that information is stored but never used.[8]

Some of the study's recommendations for remedying "Digital Diogenes Syndrome" include:

1. Be aware that the content that we save takes up space. We need to do regular cleanups.

2. Be realistic and learn to choose. We cannot know everything, so we have to know our areas of interest and focus on them.

3. Storage and indexing tools like *Delicious* can help us organize all of those interesting links that we find every day. In addition, their labeling system allows us to recover them easily if we ever need to consult them. With the rest of the content, we can use infrastructure services in the

6. See *https://en.wikipedia.org/wiki/Diogenes_syndrome.*

7. Celestino Guemes Seoane, "Beware of the Digital Diogenes Syndrome," June 6, 2012, *https://ascent.atos.net/beware-of-the-digital-diogenes-syndrome/.*

8. See *http://www.emc.com/leadership/digital-universe/2014iview/index.htm.*

cloud like *Dropbox, iCloud, Copy,* Microsoft's *Onedrive,* or *Google Drive.* However, it is not about moving information from a local support to the cloud, but of selecting what to keep and what to let go.

4. Most importantly, avoid letting the excessive bombardment of information that hits us every day overwhelm us. People often suffer stress simply because they want to take in more than what they can handle.[9]

In short, proceed with calm and lose the fear of erasing information. Before clicking on "save," think about whether the content is really necessary. Use your discretion and become friends with the "delete" key.

> Bodily obesity is corrected by watching what we eat. We can also talk about digital obesity. It is not a bad idea to go on a "digital diet" now and then to free up storage space, reduce the number of hours we dedicate to nonproductive technologies, and take a step away from our excessive attachment to video games. It is good to exercise self-control and refrain from using technological gadgets at certain times; in this way, we will keep them from becoming absolutely indispensable. Technology should be at our service; we cannot let it enslave us.

NOMOPHOBIA

People who have lost a body part, such as an arm or a leg, whether from sickness or an accident, often suffer phantom pain or a phantom itch in the area of that missing limb. For

---

9. Ibid.

those who have never suffered an amputated limb, it is very difficult to get a good idea of what it means: Where do you scratch when you have an itch in a missing leg?

> Do you notice the vibration of your cell phone even when you are not carrying it? Do you leave work and go back home to get your smartphone when you realize that you forgot it? Do you look at your screen every ten minutes in case someone sent you a message or in case you got an email or a notification from a social network?

If any of these questions hit home, then there is no doubt that you have *nomophobia*, a twenty-first century "sickness."

The term *nomophobia* is composed of *no* (negation), *mo* (cell phone), and *phobia* (irrational fear).[10] It refers to the irrational and uncontrolled fear of being separated from one's cell phone. By extension, this now applies to the fear of not being able to access emails, electronic messages, voicemail, and social networks. Nomophobia also applies to someone who cannot stop checking his email or engaging in social media activity. This interaction can take place anytime and anywhere, even if the person is not necessarily expecting an important message; there is an uncontrolled need for connections.

> Nomophobia comes from an uncontrolled and unrealistic need for connection.

---

10. See *https://en.wikipedia.org/wiki/Nomophobia*.

According to the consulted sources, it is estimated that 50 to 75 percent of cell phone users suffer some degree of nomophobia.[11] This very high level of dependency, serious in some cases, impedes or at least harms some aspects of personal freedom. It is therefore a good idea to set aside mobile devices from time to time to keep one's mobile consumption in check.

Nomophobes generally feel high stress levels, similar to the stress some feel when going to the dentist, and can easily lose their self-esteem and fall into introversion.

Aristotle said, "Nature abhors a vacuum."[12] Some artistic styles—Baroque, Rococo, some Islamic decoration, and the ostentatious Byzantine art—share this "horror of the vacuum." *Horror vacui,* which is the technical term for this form of intensive decoration of an entire pictorial or sculptural space, drives the artist not to leave a single empty spot without decoration. Nomophobia is considered the *digital horror vacui* of this century.

P2P NETWORKS

Finally, there are the P2P (peer-to-peer) networks: interactive media used by applications or networks like Ares, BitTorrent, eDonkey, Gnutella, KaZaa, and others. We do not have to demonize these networks; the architecture of their functionality is used in some commercial processes, but there are networks (like the ones mentioned above) that lend themselves to all kinds of excesses and even crimes. A

---

11. Huffington Post, "Nomophobia: 66 Percent Are Afraid to Be Separated from Cell Phones," August 8, 2012, *http://www.huffingtonpost.com/2012/05/08/nomophobia-cell-phone-addictio_n_1500670.html.*

12. Julie Ackerman, *Our Daily Bread,* January 21, 2011, *http://odb.org/2011/01/21/nature-abhors-a-vacuum/.*

P2P network allows for the direct exchange of information, in any format, between two computers connected to the Internet without any intermediary.

When people look for information via P2P, they generally do so by the catalogue name, and if they find it, they proceed to download it. Of course, no one can guarantee that what is being downloaded is what someone wanted or expected to download. For instance, we want to download a photo album of the works of art found in the Museum of Prado, but we may end up downloading a copyright-protected movie or a collection of photos depicting sexual abuse of minors? We will not know exactly what the content contains until we have downloaded it all. We should be aware that the possession of this kind of material is already a crime. Criminal images or videos are never displayed on the surface, but are kept in the backroom; on P2P, almost everything is backroom material.

Anyone, including minors, can access a P2P network, and the disadvantage is that there is no protection by content-filtering systems. P2P networks are currently the most used media for the downloading of illegal software, and they are often full of viruses. Even the downloading apps are not risk-free. If we want to protect ourselves from this, we will have to employ user-based filtering software that monitors the connections of P2P networks, as well as the Web navigation itself. In a home environment, if we do not need a P2P network, why would we allow it? The exposure to risk would be as high as it is useless. My advice is to never install P2P apps on a minor's computer without a sufficiently justified need for it.

REMEMBER:

1. The same qualities that make mobile devices so valuable (the here-and-now aspect) also make it more possible for people to become overly dependent on them.

2. The use of tablets or smartphones as educational tools can be a double-edged sword that ends up leading to scholastic failure.

3. Digital Diogenes Syndrome (the accumulation of useless digital information), nomophobia (the irrational fear of being separated from one's cell phone), compulsive behavior (leading to social isolation), and Blackberry Thumb are current and habitual issues caused by using mobile devices in an unsuitable way.

5

THE INTERNET

SAYING THE WORD *INTERNET* IS SIMILAR to saying nothing, which is about the same as saying everything. Some time ago, you often heard people justify a statement with the argument that "I heard it on TV." That was enough of a reason to validate that a piece of information, a guideline, or medical tip was true. Television no longer has the power of yesteryear, although it does remain influential. Its position has been replaced to some degree by the Internet. Now Google is our favorite way to find out what happened, how to interpret events, or what diet we should follow. It is even used as a verb, synonymous with seeking information on the Web, as in "Google it."

> Freedom is the fundamental characteristic of the Internet.

The Internet was born as a free interconnection network. Freedom is one of its essential characteristics. In fact, some attempts to limit the freedom of the Internet have caused a tremendous social clash between the technical and political communities.

We should not confuse the Internet with the Web. The World Wide Web, www, or simply the Web uses the Internet as a means of access, but the Web is not the entire Internet. The Web is a system of hyperlinked information: texts, images, and videos that require a very simple form of operation. One starts a navigation session and then clicks on the hyperlinks to jump from one document to another. We can navigate on the Web, and we can also surf. And if you don't know how to swim, you can drown.

The Internet, on the other hand, is a data transport network. It is already fairly old, but it has been updated over time. It allows for the interconnection of all computers or devices that have a connection to one of its access points, typically an Internet network. This network hosts Web servers and many other services.

Users can gain access to the Internet by using other connection networks. For example, we can connect to the Internet by using telephone landlines, cell phone networks (such as 3G and 4G), DSL (digital subscriber line) access points, or cable. Thus almost any electronic device can obtain an Internet connection from almost anywhere.

Telephone companies typically offer their clients, in a single contract, the integrated aggregate of many services, frequently at a flat fee. Thus, any client of these companies can talk on the phone (telephone service), navigate on the Internet (data service), or receive SMS (short message services) with a single contract. The service is always available when the operator's network is reachable (within the coverage zone). If it is not the case, for example, because one has moved to a foreign country, the phone might try to connect to an alternate network of another company (international roaming), which makes the rates go up steeply and changes what was once a flat fee. We should take this into account when we travel to another country, and we should also warn our children about it if we do not want a surprise on our return from our trip, with a bill showing a lot of extra zeros in the wrong place.

Most of the data hosted on the Internet is out of the reach of ordinary Web surfers, meaning that the data is not linked in or the access links are not available to the general public because the search engines do not index them. This is known as the Deep Internet. It is estimated that 90 percent of the information stored on the Internet belongs to its hidden side.[1]

The information on the Deep Internet is quite varied. It may contain documents with information against the law, manuals on how to carry out attacks—in general, criminal data. Not all of the hidden Internet is that way; it also holds commercial and business information that companies want to have online, but not accessible to the public.

Anyone happening to access this information will have little protection, since unknown pages (not indexed by the search engines, for example) won't appear on the content filters' lists of prohibited pages.

> Another interesting fact: It is estimated that 25 percent of the entire content of the Web is pornographic. No, that is not an error: 25 percent of the visible Internet, not the deep Web. How can we defend ourselves from this overwhelming reality? Isn't it worthwhile to take this seriously? To get the most out of the immense potential of the Internet, must we abandon our cultural and moral standards? The answer is a resound-

---

1. Peter J. Denning and Craig Martell, *Great Principles of Computing* (Cambridge, MA: MIT Press, 2015) p. 132.

> ing no. Instead, we must learn to make the most of all its advantages, getting everything we can out of them, and explore ways to defend ourselves from the threats and risks that this medium brings.

THE THREE VERSIONS OF THE WEB

We said earlier that referring to the *Web* as opposed to the *Internet* is too broad to mean anything. In fact, the Web has evolved over the years, and there are now three versions: 1, 2, and 3. We are now in version 2 (or 2.0), and we are moving toward version 3.

- Web 1, or just "the Web," is the traditional Web with pages of static information posted on Web servers that can be browsed via a navigator. The risk of this Web modality is twofold: (1) what information the pages contain, and (2) what we can download from them. Since they are static pages, they can easily be filtered, so it is relatively easy to offer protection against any inappropriate content. As for the downloads of files from this Web, we can only defend ourselves from viruses or malware if we have our up-to-date antivirus software, which is crucial and much more important than what it may seem at first glance. However, it will not protect us from inappropriate content included in downloaded files. Nor will it protect us from attacks that come from encrypted or password-protected files.

- The next version of the Web is called Web 2.0, or the social Web. In this case, what is added to version 1 is *sociability*, which means that users can generate information through digital socialization. Thus, the pages are no longer static, but are organically built through the information that visitors add to them. Web 2.0 includes social networks, whose pages are constantly growing. In addition to the risks of Web 1, there are new ones: Web 2.0 invites new addictions and allows new forms of virtual but direct relationships that require monitoring, especially in the case of people with immature character formation. We will go over this in more detail later when we cover the social networks.

• Finally, the newest Web modality is 3.0, also called the semantic Web. In this case, search engines or other Web services are given semantic intelligence, which facilitates an interactive language close to the human one. The semantic Web is a great technical advance, but it lends itself to manipulation, and therefore, its risks—more ideological than anything else—come from twisting the answers to users' search requests or to following their digital trail.

THE INTERNET OF THINGS AND VIRTUAL REALITY

The "Internet of Things" is the term given to the construction of a global network that uses the Internet as an intercommunication network to connect daily objects to each other. The idea is to connect any device or object with value to the Internet.

For example, domestic appliances in our home soon will be connected to the Internet, allowing us to manipulate them remotely from our cell phones. Not only home devices, either, but also our clothing, which will come equipped with controls to play music and an Internet connection to download music. Even sunglasses will have Internet connections and will be able to give us information in real time about the visual reality we are observing. For example, when we pass by a restaurant, our sunglasses will let us know when it opens and closes, its list of prices, the house specialty, and so on. It's all part of the virtual, or augmented, reality.

This all might sound like science fiction, but all of the examples I have mentioned are real and already exist, at least as prototypes. From here on, there are no limits to the imagination. If we think about this reality, we quickly realize that the Internet is not a technology that we can just put in parentheses. The fact that it cannot be dismissed is the reason why this book was written.

IP VOICE SERVICES

It's true that the Internet is a huge data transport network that can be accessed from any device. On the other hand, the conventional telephone, whether via landline or mobile line, is a costly voice transport service. So why not digitize the voice and transport it over the Internet, knowing this will be a free service if we have a flat rate for accessing the Internet (which is usually the case)? The technology that does this is called IP telephony or IP voice services (technically, VoIP, which stands for Voice over Internet Protocol).

You do not need a phone to use VoIP as long as you have a device that connects to the Internet and has a microphone, a speaker, and software that provides the functionality of a telephone. Thus, you can have a phone conversation using a smartphone, a digital tablet, or a personal computer. This means that the telephone as such is no longer a concrete, physical device; now it is a computer application (i.e., Skype, Google Hangouts) or a specific app on a tablet or smartphone. And all for free, since it would be included in the basic Internet access fee.

These services provide electronic messaging and video conferencing using a device's video camera. This is always dangerous, especially if the users are children or minors, because a video camera shows everything that is in front of it. Cyber-stalkers use social networks, chat rooms, and associated messaging and video conferencing systems as their favorite vehicles to commit crimes. However, these same vehicles also offer interesting characteristics that can be very useful—such as in education, business, or customer service.

> In any case, having a virtually free telephone service that is always available is a serious threat for our concentration, because if we are not careful, we will always be distracted by the mobile phone. The guidance departments of high schools and universities already warn of the correlation between the intensive use of cell phones and the lack of concentration in cognitive processes. Only prudent moderation can free us from this danger. Mobility should always go hand in hand with responsibility.

REMEMBER:

1. The main characteristic of the Internet is freedom.
2. It is estimated that 25 percent of the information on the Internet is pornographic.
3. We are now in the midst of Web 2.0, in which the user is a content creator.
4. There is a relationship between the indiscriminate use of mobile devices and the lack of concentration in cognitive functions.

6

___ . ___

SECURITY ON THE INTERNET

EXPERIENCE HAS SHOWN THAT IF WE do not voluntarily expose ourselves to danger, we will significantly reduce the risk of getting hurt. This is basically true, but with TICs (Trusted Internet Connections) it is not the whole truth: On the Internet, even if you do not expose yourself, danger still lurks. While we should not let the potential threats keep us from using its services, we should still put an emphasis on prevention.

The organizations that are dedicated to studying the security of computer systems and processes recommend working in technological areas that are protected with *in-depth defense* strategies. For the general public, this means that the systems (devices, programs, services, communications) require intensive protection on all levels, in such a way that every one of them applies whatever is needed to safeguard the user's security. If a firewall is brought down, another one

> On the Internet, it is not enough to avoid exposing yourself to risk. You have to protect yourself.

appears behind it that sets up some obstacle, and then another and another.

But we should not fall into an obsessive paranoia of wanting to eliminate all risks. No matter how much we may try to guarantee a process, there will always be some possibility of exposure to an attack. The security of a chain of processes is a matter of the security of the weakest link.

Let us consider an example of in-depth defense:

> To protect children from accessing pornographic pages, some parents decided to install a content-filtering system that they have configured correctly. From then on, a high percentage of pages were correctly blocked (there is always a small percentage that the filter fails to block). However, the possibility of making connections to P2P networks, which are not usually controlled by the content-blocking systems, remains. If the parents want security on the P2P connections, they have to be protected by additional firewalls.
>
> Even though the parents have increased the security, family members can download files that can contain a virus. To protect themselves from this new threat, they will have to install antivirus software.
>
> Now a family member wants to make a purchase on the Internet, so he or she goes to the virtual store and is asked for a credit card to make the electronic payment. Of course, the page seems to be authentic, but it might not be (phishing) and if so, the family member would be giving his or her bank information to someone who should not have it. Now, to avoid these types of attacks, the parents will need to have an anti-phishing system.

> This can continue on almost indefinitely. We can-
> not live in a state of constant alert, but that's what
> in-depth defense is all about.

Fortunately, commercial security solutions for home use usually protect us for a modest price from all those threats, but the antivirus software with anti-phishing, firewalls, and content blockers must be constantly updated. In other words, it is not enough to buy and install it; we have to update it and keep it running continuously.

The attacks mentioned in the previous pages are associated with the user's activity. However, other attacks come from without and have nothing to do with the user's input. These are sophisticated attacks, but easy to launch and not infrequent, especially within organizations. The risks of these attacks come from failing to update the operating systems of the computers or mobile devices, or not updating the apps installed on them. If the apps are legal, there should be no problem managing the updates. But if they are pirated, users will not be able to update them, which seriously increases the risk level. Legal soft-ware (which can sometimes be free) is always profitable from a security standpoint.

THE MAIN EXPOSURES TO RISK
ON THE HOME FRONT

Here is a brief list of the main exposures to risk in the home, small office environment, or educational setting. Sometimes malware cannot be definitively classified into only one of the following types, since a single infected application can have multiple adverse effects.

- **Viruses.** A virus is a program (or fragment of a program) running as a malicious activity that includes the propagation of other programs in the same or another computer. The malicious activities could include capturing sensitive information and sending it to an external point programmed in advance by the virus developer, or launching another unexpected application (for example, launching the navigator toward a specific page), or destroying information, or preventing connections to Internet sites that offer disinfection tools. Antivirus programs can prevent computer viruses from propagating. These programs also disinfect, but not always as effectively as we would like. Antivirus software must be installed while the computer is still clean; it is almost useless if it is already infected, although there are sophisticated procedures to use in this situation.

- **Spyware.** Similar to viruses, their function is to monitor the users' activity in order to send information to an outside recipient about that activity, which the attacker can then use for his own benefit. A particular form of spyware is the key-logger application, which captures the keys users type as a way to get useful information such as passwords, credit card numbers, and so on. Most antivirus programs include anti-spyware to prevent the uncontrolled leaking of information.

Users need to be aware that by accepting a licensing agreement with an application's provider, they enter into a relationship with that provider. The licensor will capture some information on the licensee. This is not a problem with a reputable vendor. However, users should be very careful when installing free apps, because by accepting the license, they may open themselves to a "legal" attack. An unscrupulous provider of certain free apps will use the licensee's information for purposes to the detriment of the user.

- **Phishing.** This involves posing as something that one is not and using techniques of deception to get the attacked user to reveal his passwords, bank accounts, pin numbers, and credit card numbers. Security suites usually include phishing detectors along with antivirus and anti-spyware. Later we will provide some advice for avoiding the possibility of this type of attack.

- **Spam.** Spamming means indiscriminately sending unsolicited email. As such, it is not an attack, but is a waste the recipient's time, who has to delete the message after reading it. It is estimated that eight out of every ten emails are spam. This leads to major losses for the Internet companies, which have fewer resources to dedicate to their clients when they are uselessly caught up in spam traffic.

- **Wi-Fi intercepting.** Wireless networks (Wi-Fi, Bluetooth) do not require massive cabling systems to maintain their transmissions, since they do it over radio waves that are spread out in space around the antennas. This means that any recipient situated in the coverage area of the emitting antenna will be able to hear (in technical jargon, "sniff") the communication. If the communicated messages are not encrypted, anyone can violate their confidentiality. Thus, the access points usually encrypt the connections, but not all encryption methods are equally effective. A Wi-Fi connection must always be encrypted with WPA[1], WPA2, or higher. The WEP[2] encryption method should not be used, since it is extremely easy to break.

---

1. Wi-Fi Protected Access.
2. Wired Equivalent Privacy.

- **Social engineering attacks.** In this case, the attacker tries to fool the users so that they reveal something that they would never intentionally disclose. Sometimes, because of the victim's naiveté and lack of caution, it is not even necessary to do anything to carry out the deception. We should never choose passwords that can be found in any language's dictionary, to avoid "dictionary attacks." Passwords with only a few characters are also weak, because they lend themselves to "brute attacks." It is not a good idea to create passwords that a hypothetical attacker could guess, such as one's date of birth or wedding date, the name of one's spouse, or similar information. Users should always choose strong passwords and never use the same password for all services. A password should always be protected from the sight of others, and it should never be written somewhere where it could easily be lost. We should certainly know the passwords used by our children, which we can verify by frequently sharing browsing sessions with them.

7

SOCIAL NETWORKS

SOCIAL NETWORKS ARE THE CORE NUCLEUS of the Web 2.0, since their idiosyncrasy is based on the creative activity of the users who take part in them.

Participation is always interesting, but we should ask ourselves some concrete questions: Participation in what? Participation to relate to whom? And how? When? Where? For what reason?

Many teachers complain about their students' lack of participation in class. Teaching plans thus often end up focusing on stimulating the active participation of the students. In the lesson planning for the different subjects, the teachers plan activities with the goal of getting students to form relationships with each other and learn to debate or respect others' opinions, even though they may be different from their own. Participation is good, and the Internet invites us to do it through tools that stimulate the active involvement of its users.

> If you are a parent, how many times have you warned your kids not to talk to strangers? So then, why don't you follow that advice when the relationship is established on the Internet, knowing that the medium

protects the anonymity of the potential predator? I hope this question has put you on guard.

WHAT IS A SOCIAL NETWORK?

A social network represents a particular social structure in which there are relationships between the members in accordance with some specific criteria. These relationships build the structure of the society they represent. This is not a new idea, but what is original is its application to cybernetic relationship environments, which is why we call them online social networks. Today social networks can be accessed from any device that can be connected to the Internet, not just from a personal computer. In fact, most social network users connect from their smartphones.

You join a social network by filling out an online form with some personal information, which then becomes more or less public. This information usually includes your name and email address, although you can also choose to provide other information, such as your date of birth and where you live. If you have recently joined the social network, you will be able to configure the visibility of your personal information, but you have to know how to do this. The procedure varies from one network to another.

Parents and educators have to teach the minors in their care how to set up the visibility of their personal information on the social networks, helping them to value their own privacy and that of others.

In any case, the social network's home page usually includes a link to a page showing the user how to configure the privacy of his or her personal information. The problem is that many users never consult this page and do not worry about privacy, which is a boon for those who want to do damage. There is no way of ensuring on a social network that the person who contacts us is who he says he is, so we are in constant danger of dealing with fake identities. On the one hand, someone can usurp our identity to fool other people, and on the other, someone can usurp the identity of a person we know in order to fool us. Meanwhile those who victimize users of social media can manipulate the Internet to protect their anonymity, and thus crimes can remain unpunished because of the difficulty of identifying those who commit them.

Before we publish information on a social network, we should stop and think, because once it is published, we will no longer have any control over what we have written. We should not forget the traditional saying: "We are masters of what we keep to ourselves and slaves of what we say." It is also smart to control the list of contacts that we allow to relate to us. We should not accept new contacts that we do not know or with whom we have no personal relationship apart from the Internet. Finally, we should be aware of the privacy policies of the social networks we choose and their terms of use. If not, we could be in for some unpleasant surprises.

HOW MANY SOCIAL NETWORKS ARE THERE TODAY?

There are countless social networks of many different kinds. The Wikipedia page that lists these networks continues to grow. I suggest that the reader consult this page[1] to read more about the main characteristics of each social network.

---

1. See *https://en.wikipedia.org/wiki/List_of_social_networking_websites*.

Most of the influential social networks are now inter-connected, so if a user publishes a message or document on one of them, it will be automatically or semi-automatically published on other networks on which we are also registered. This enables the quick spread of information, but it also produces an information overload that can cause problems, which we will discuss later.

The most used networks include:

- **Tuenti.** This is a Spanish social network that operates internationally. Although it was originally intended for university students, and registration required an invitation by one of its members, it was later opened up to any user over the age of eleven, although there is no way of verifying the user's age in the initial electronic registration. Most Tuenti users today are very young and use the social network as a means of social interaction: making plans to go out, chatting, playing with other users in real time, sharing photos and videos, and sending private messages between registered users.

- **Twitter.** Twitter is actually a microblogging service based out of California with a worldwide following. The network allows users to send messages (tweets) with a maximum of 140 characters as if they were articles (posts) on a blog that can be read publicly. Publication notifications, about what any other user publishes on Twitter, are automatic available for subscribers (followers). Each user can subscribe to as many Twitter users as she wants. In addition to writing messages, users can post photos, videos, and links to Web pages. By default, the messages are public, although there can also be private messages between a user and his or her followers. It is estimated that 40 percent of Twitter messages do not have any relevance, and another 20 percent share repeated messages (retweets), spam, or advertising. Twitter has had an overwhelming social impact; in fact, it is one of the most visited pages on the Internet.

- **Facebook.** Also originating from a university setting, Facebook was created for the students at Harvard University but eventually was opened up to include anyone, with the sole requirement of registering with an email address. It is now one of the most visited pages on the Internet. On Facebook, one's contacts are called friends, and it offers services like lists of friends, chats, timeline updates (on one's own timeline or on those of friends), the ability to have groups of friends, create fan pages, post photos, offer gifts, advertise products, show interests (by hitting "like" or "favorites"), play games, and more. Concerning the protection of minors, Facebook created a panic button—a Web application that allows a minor to get in touch with administrators who are authorized to intervene if signs of abuse are detected.

- **LinkedIn.** This website was created to build professional networks. It was the first American social network to go public on the New York Stock Exchange and is the largest network in the world for professionals. The network is built by inviting other users with whom one maintains or would like to maintain some kind of professional relationship. Within the network, the invited person can accept or reject the connection and also can report it as spam or as an unknown connection. If a user sends a lot of spam to his connections, his LinkedIn account can be restricted or even shut down. LinkedIn is a fairly serious network and is widely used to find work or look for people with a specific professional profile. Users can list their resumes and design their own professional profiles. The visibility of their data can also be adjusted, although it is better—given the network's professional character—to make almost all the information on one's profile public and accessible, at least to one's contacts and professional recruiters.

- **Google+.** Also called Google Plus or G+, this is Google's social network. Users have to be over age thirteen to register. It offers many services, but the most important thing to note is that Google+ is more than a social network, since through the integrated Google services, we are giving this enormous company information about what we do on social networks, in our emails, and in our browsers. Google+ also allows for video conferencing or interactive sessions (hangouts), so if we use this network, we can create our own presentations directly. This is widely used in the educational area, but it's also frequented by stalkers. Users can organize their contacts into groups ("circles" in G+ terminology) with whom they share specific information in a particular way. It also includes educational apps, instant messaging, news, recommendations, social games, email, tasks, and shared documents. Google+ is a universe of interconnected services that continues to grow.

- **Instagram.** Developed as a photography application for cell phones, Instagram is a social network for publishing one's own photos. Every photo taken with the application through the cell phone can be retouched with one of the many photographic filters and then published on one's own social network or on Facebook and Twitter. Instagram is one of the fastest-growing networks and the basis of many photo blogs.

- **Pinterest.** This social network allows users to share images (known as *pins*), categorizing them into personal thematic boards or collections of images related to some event, interest, or hobby. Its objective is to connect all its members through shared interests. In fact, the term Pinterest comes from *pins* and *interest*.

- **StumbleUpon.** A commercial Web page, StumbleUpon is connected to a social network. Registered users can exchange the addresses of Web pages of interest, classifying them by topic.

- **Flickr.** Registered users publish, organize, and sell photographs and videos on this Web page. The system allows for labeling and commenting on users' photos. There is both a free version and a paid version.

- **Tumblr.** A microblogging platform, Tumblr allows users to publish various documents, texts, images, videos, and audios. Some users can follow the content that others post by registering as followers, a process that allows for a high degree of personalization.

- **Edmodo.** This is a free educational social microblogging network that facilitates communication between teachers and students in a closed and private environment, so it is fairly secure and applicable to educational environments. It allows users to create groups, publish, send, and receive messages, share documents and links, post grades, send homework to students, and access materials, news, and events.

REMEMBER:

1. The great danger of a social network is that it protects the anonymity of a hypothetical criminal.
2. Participation is good, and the Internet invites users to participate through tools that stimulate their active involvement.
3. It is up to parents and educators to teach minors to protect their own privacy and that of others.

8

THE BLOGOSPHERE
AND THE NEW PEDAGOGIES

A BLOG, OR ELECTRONIC LOG, is a dynamic Web page structured according to a chronological sequence. Most of the information created on the Internet is publicly presented in the form of blogs. When a user accesses a blog, he or she can locate information that is organized sequentially by the date of publication. The articles published on a blog are called posts. The blogosphere is the entirety of all of the blogs on the Web.

Bloggers' posts are usually labeled under categories and with tags that describe their topic, which makes it easy to search for articles related to a specific topic; the chronological order of the blog thus becomes secondary. Internet services such as Delicious are dedicated to offering these labeling systems, classifying the articles, and thereby becoming thematic organizers of the blogosphere.

At the end of each article, the blog owner usually sets up an area where readers can leave comments and suggestions. The commenters can be identified by their user names or, if the blogger permits, can remain anonymous. This way of organizing content—composed of the original post, classification labels, and comments—allow readers to enter into conversation with each other, creating a discussion forum on the article's topic. It is also very common for blogs to be associated with social networks; when a blog reader reads a post, he or she can publish it automatically on the social networks to which he or she belongs, thus giving the post a wider audience.

Blogs are popular because of their simple structure, and the fact that they are easy to set up. Some Internet companies—such as Wordpress or Blogger—offer free services for blog creation, as well as simple tools so that even those without advanced programming know-how can create a blog based on some predefined templates and simple instructions.

Since visual images and videos are very attractive, many bloggers have created blogs that focus on them. These are called photo blogs or video blogs. These types of blogs are very easy to peruse, since they have no text. When people—especially children and youth—get used to consuming only this type of visual information, they may relax their textual consumption to the point that they feel a certain aversion for reading because of the added effort that text requires. Visual information is very striking and effective—a picture is worth a thousand words—but a steady diet of it weakens our capacity to read and understand text.

Here are some recommendations and precautions regarding blogs.

- **Identity of the blog.** The blog can be identified by its owner through public information displayed on the blog, although there are also blogs in which one person is the owner (the manager) and others are authors of the articles. It is a recommended practice for blog articles to be signed so their authorship can be identified.

Unsigned articles do not merit trust. Signed posts can be trusted insofar as the author is trustworthy. Be aware— the writer and publisher are not necessarily the same person.

- **Respect for authors' rights.** All of the published material on a blog should be the author's original work, or at least he or she should have publication rights to the material. Sometimes all or part of the information comes from another source. In this case, bloggers should be careful to identify where it comes from by citing the source. If an article features images, bloggers should also respect the reproduction rights of the image used. Many photo libraries on the Internet are intended for public use.

- **Use appropriate language.** Since many people will probably read the information published on a blog, the language used must not be aggressive or violent. Someone who visits a blog should be pleasantly informed of whatever is being communicated but should never feel violated or insulted. Bloggers should take care to always maintain the basic rules of courtesy, especially because on the Internet everything is registered forever. Neglecting these little details leads to creating a sordid and unpleasant *digital reputation*. Good manners are a social virtue that also applies to the Internet.

- **Respect others' opinions.** Readers should be especially respectful in discussion forums or on comments pages, both on blogs and on the various social networks. If someone opens a public discussion topic, that person should be aware that he or she has opened the door to opposing opinions. No matter how well a person argues his or her point, there will always be someone who disagrees. Pejorative comments should be eliminated, or at least softened. This also applies to the answers bloggers write to those who comment on their posts.

THE PROBLEM OF INFOXICATION

It's important to have information. It's much more important to have *good* information. We can also have too much information, with insufficient time to analyze it, hence rendering it useless. When we do not have enough information to make a decision, we end up choosing with less prudence, a key virtue that is so necessary for organizing our life in the right way. An imprudent decision, either due to insufficient or excessive information, surrenders our success to pure chance.

The Internet offers a great deal of information of all topics and viewpoints and from many sources. However, with social networks or the blogosphere, much of the information is extremely tenuous. Most of the content people create on the social networks is absolutely irrelevant.

Having more information than we can analyze is useless.

The information seems trivial; yet social networks are frequently used to statistically analyze the importance of a piece of information or a commercial product during its launch phase. For example, let's say someone publishes on his Facebook timeline that a certain trendy singer just launched a new CD. His Facebook friends will read the news, and perhaps someone among them, who does not like that type of music, will proposes something else, making some comment such as, "This performer is very old-fashioned. We listen to this other singer instead." Next, the singers' fans will hit "like" for the option that best fits their personal tastes. If the debate is interesting to people, more comments will ensue, followed by more "likes" and causing a viral process of rapid expansion through the Internet. This lasts for a period of time, usually a quite short time. Afterward the debate will be quickly forgotten and the matter absolutely obsolete.

As you can see, none of the information posted on that Facebook timeline was memorable. The published news, although it might have been interesting, was useful only for the consumption of the moment. The relationships between those who commented or approved the publication were very superficial. The purpose was never to reach a conclusion by argument. The process was fairly useless for the Facebook users and had no long-term impact.

But the record company now does have valuable information about the consumption habits and preferences of those who participated, and that information will guide the way the CD is marketed.

The users who participated in the discussion may feel very satisfied because of the high degree of participation, but having a lot of Facebook friends, who participate in a discussion, is really only comparable to playing a game using a lot of Monopoly money.

This example is fictitious but it brings out an important point: Not everything published is necessarily information worth retaining; not everything contributes lasting value. But the problem does not end here. It is also often difficult to guarantee that the published information is reliable and true, especially because a great deal of the content published on the Internet is unsigned and of unknown origin. While a signature does not make the information true, it does serve as a guide. Most of the information found on many blogs was not created by the one who published it, but often consists of material copied from other sites. Internet technology facilitates a lot of this hypermedia composition, which is why we say we "surf" the Web.

Therefore, a first word of caution: The statements we find on the Internet are not necessarily true. This lack of veracity is not necessarily due to someone deliberately wanting to fool us, but often to inaccuracies and false supposition in the information transmitted by the publisher and our own lack of knowledge about the topic.

> Because of the virality[1] that can be achieved on the Internet, a false report can eventually seem true. And since information is also consumed at high speeds, it is difficult for us to use good judgment—we can easily end up thinking that all news is equally important, or perhaps not at all important. This creates a kind of information numbness and a relaxation of the healthy critical spirit we should all have, which can easily lead us to become victims of misinformation or manipulation of information.

If we choose any topic and start looking for information about it on the Internet, we find very diverse opinions with very different agendas. A healthy critical sense will lead us to discriminate between the sources of those opinions, the importance of each of them, and the weight of the argumentation on which they are based. This is part of the

---

1. Virality is the propensity for online information to circulate quickly and widely from one user to other users, i.e. "going viral."

scientific method. However, if we find ourselves with too much information for the time we have to analyze it, we can experience a certain intellectual anxiety caused by information overload—something that has been called *infobesity* or *infoxication*.

Our mind reacts to that anxiety by employing a psychological self-defense that takes the form of intellectual anesthesia. Both the infoxication and the resulting numbness are highly damaging to a scientific analysis of data and for getting to the bottom of realities. We could say that this situation, generated by a lack of critical spirit, leads to a new form of relativism that is no substitute for truth. From an anthropological point of view, we can say that if we do not know the truth, we cannot achieve love. Without love, we cannot be happy.

> Why did we delve into the depths of anthropology in the paragraphs above? If we are not aware of these realities, we will be exposed to major changes in our perception of life, without freely agreeing to them and without even being fully aware of the change. When the first cracks in the surface of our life appear, we can intuit that perhaps it is because the subterranean currents have washed away the intellectual and moral subsoil. We realize that the Internet is full of subterranean rivers. If you realize that you are cracking, explore your subsoil, lest you drown in your own ground water table.

THE NEW DIGITAL INTERNET SKILLS

Right now, the Internet is an integral part of the digital human's DNA. Most of the modern human population, almost anywhere in the world, has left behind digital illiteracy, because the world is now full of digital natives, or at least digital immigrants.

New times have brought new ways, and these in turn have brought new tools. The novelty of the tools requires new skills. And since the world is massively digital, the skills required now are digital. All of this, translated into real life, means that we cannot hide behind irrational excuses. We have to take the necessary steps to acquire these digital skills and not lose the opportunity to relate to what the Internet and its galaxy of services offers us; that is, we have to become, at the very least, digital immigrants.

Most professional activities today have some digital component, without which the professional task would be very different, if not deeply downgraded. The professional profile demanded in many work roles requires some or various digital competencies; if we ignore this fact, we will cut ourselves off from many employment prospects.

For example, many schools now communicate with their students' parents or tutors through messaging or email. They also publish the dates of their students' exams and homework information on classroom blogs so parents can check them. Parents can check absentee lists as well as their children's grades through the school website, and they set up interviews with tutors through a shared digital calendar. If we think about it, in order to be good parents in today's world, we need to have at least some digital skills.

Since many schools organize educational content by using a teaching method that includes computers and tablets, it is vitally important for our children to have or acquire these digital skills. If not, they will feel out of place in the classroom. It is usually not particularly difficult for kids to start acquiring digital competency, since they are the best suited to become "digital natives," but there are children who have more difficulty learning these skills.

THE NEW PEDAGOGIES: CONSTRUCTIVISM AND CONNECTIVISM

A good part of an educator's work changes when the school decides to integrate technology into its curriculum. In the School 2.0, the protagonist is the student with his device. In this school model, teachers generally follow a *constructivist pedagogy*: The teacher has a new function similar to what some call *content curation*. This basically means that the teacher dedicates his or her time to selecting the material the students will study online. This curating process is also, in some way, a new function of the parents, since there is not much of a difference between the classroom and the home with these pedagogical methods. The main competence a professor must have to be a good content curator is critical sense: not just for organizing a way to defend students from unwanted Internet content, but also to avoid *infoxicating* students with a downpour of possibilities that bury them under tons of digital sediments.

> Since we are going to be surrounded by technology and the Internet eventually will be integrated into all of our activity, we have to take seriously everything that is connected to the Internet. Our professions, education, moral life, relationships with others, and even our health are all going the way of the Internet. If we do not get with the Internet program, we will be as irresponsible as someone who jumps in without taking any precautions whatsoever. If we abandon prudence, then prudence will abandon us.

In the modern world, the new pedagogies that are used in many schools use Internet-enabled devices that are basically digital tablets and computers, although they may also be cell phones and video game consoles. Pedagogical constructivism affirms that knowledge is built through relationships that a student establishes with his surroundings. It is about a learning process. But does constructivism lead to truth?

The problem becomes even keener when constructivism advances toward *connectivism*, in which greater weight is given to the relationships between people who share the learning process. For example, students can learn through their mutual relationship over the social networks, discussion forums, and other services that allow for participation. This fosters activity, improves attitudes, develops certain values, and teaches them to respect others' opinions. But does it help them to learn the truth? Who guarantees that at the end of this learning process, the students will have acquired true knowledge?

> An adult has enough of a critical sense to draw his own conclusions from the opinions expressed in a forum, but a child does not. An imprudent connection could lead the child to mental confusion; it can lead him to think that all information expressed and discussed has the same value, and that is an error. All opinions deserve respect, but not all are true. In this sense, immoderate connectivism opens the door to a certain relativism, which flourishes in the mobile technology environment. The source from which this relativism is supplied is the Internet.

THE TROJAN HORSE OF TECHNOLOGY

Technology acts as a vehicle for many active agents that are not always harmless. It is relatively easy to tell if someone already has a technological addiction; it is enough to watch them. However, we are not always aware of the other risks that come into our lives in the same way the Greeks entered Troy, hidden inside a wooden horse. These risks become especially important when the field of technological action is in education or formation in general.

At the start of the eighteenth century, the Italian philosopher Giambattista Vico developed the "*'verum factum'* principle." The essence of his thinking is captured in two phrases: "*verum ipsum factum* (truth lies in achievement)" and "*verum factum convertum* (truth and achievement are convertible)."[2]

According to Vico, "knowing is a process of construction or constitution and that the maker alone has the fullest knowledge about that which he or she created."[3] This has vitally important consequences for education, because "makers or creators can know what they make."[4] Vico's philosophy sinks its roots into a deep skepticism, which bears fruit in the dominant relativism of today's postmodern culture.

That "to do-to know" equation is the famous *know-how* of today's pedagogical techniques in learning by skills, which is so highly valued in corporations and business schools.

---

2. New World Encyclopedia contributors, "Giambattista Vico," New World Encyclopedia, *http://www.newworldencyclopedia.org/p/index.php?title=Giambattista_Vico&oldid=976988* (accessed May 2016).

3. Ibid.

4. Ibid.

Learning by doing is certainly valuable. But the confusion of knowledge (the ontological truth in one's intellect) with the cognitive process used to apprehend it is problematic. It is not a good idea to scorn acquired know-how, but it must be taken off its pedestal.

The idolatry of know-how, which is proper to the utilitarian mentality, is one of the many paths that lead to relativism. The operative habits it generates unconsciously are impressive. For example, 70 percent of tablet users wait only two seconds for a Web page to open. If it takes longer, they abandon it.

> What does all of this have to do with the topic of this book? Much more than it may seem. We have already seen that mobile technologies promote production and learning environments based on the relationship (something that is established, that is done), where the people matter less than the relationship in itself (part of constructivism). The information is not as important as the way in which it is consumed. The same can apply to the tendency to make our own content, because only what I build is truly trustworthy or useful. We see yet again that a lot of information (the entire Internet) produces a huge lack of information: that is, we run the risk of infoxicating both our intellect and our will.

In e-learning (learning through electronic media and new technologies), the teacher not only does not vanish, but gains new energy, because the teacher has to acquire new teaching skills. The teacher using the new technologies loses part of her direct relationship with the student, but in exchange she acquires many other educational possibilities that the traditional teacher could never realize. However, if all the teacher cares about is know-how, then formation is reduced to acquiring a collection of skills, while the acquisition of intellectual habits is set aside and the development of a critical sense is weakened. Thus, these new technology-driven teaching techniques demand both boldness and prudence to constructively integrate traditional and proven approaches with new developments.

Now we are ready to understand in greater depth the stunning effect of the novelty of the social networks and the new digital syndromes that the psychologists and psychiatrists have begun to diagnose. Are the social networks dangerous, and are the new teaching methodologies useless? Not necessarily. Are they harmless? Not that either. We do not have to ask more of Wikipedia than what it can give.

From the educational perspective, the most logical approach is to make better use of the traditional methods and of those based on technology. Why would we uproot one of them when both are beneficial? Some very new pedagogies exclude traditional methods, but the most natural and logical tendency is what we now call hybrid education, or *blended learning.*

Blended learning seeks to combine the methods of in-person education with online learning, both in and outside of the classroom, in order to improve the student's learning experience. This method uses videos, challenges, open classrooms, external activities, social networks, and the creation and publishing of content. Hybrid education allows the educational material to be more dynamic and accessible, since the student can choose his or her way of learning. However, it is a huge challenge for teachers, since they must develop their digital competencies, help the students in real time, prepare the classes dynamically based on the momentary activity of their students, and so on.

In the methodology of flipped classrooms, the students study the digital content at home, according to what is assigned by the teachers (who act as content curators) or according to what they search for. They then use their time in the classroom to discuss together or in groups, reach conclusions together, clear up differences, and build new content based on what they studied.

But there is a Trojan horse. Since the main educational element is no longer the teacher but the student, who guarantees that the student will follow the guidelines set out for learning? And if the student does not follow them, how can the teacher convince him or her to do so?

The new learning methods are emotionally captivating. Most of the time they get students more interested in the educational activities, but no one can guarantee that this will be the case for all students and in all subjects.

In another field, that of the games, we find another Trojan horse. The culture of computer games is expanding in an unstoppable way. There are continually more games available, and now there are more players of all ages and more types of mobile devices for playing. Educational games have such motivational power that they have become important tools for teaching students.

A problem occurs when we use the same term to refer to recreational games and educational games. We can fall into the mistake of thinking they are the same, when the only thing they share is the motivational mechanism. Thus, when a school proposes learning based on a computer game, it must be checked carefully to see exactly what it does, what games it uses, and what objectives it pursues. In other words, games, like educational apps, must be integrated in a carefully developed pedagogical plan, preferably one of proven effectiveness. Unfortunately, the educational game developers do not usually provide statistics on the educational effectiveness of their products. And neither do the schools that use them.

There are studies that show that the use of educational technology generally improves the learning process, although it does not necessarily raise students' grades, mainly because of the lack of methodological coordination between what is learned and what is evaluated. In most cases, educational technology relaxes the internal memory with which we think and express concepts and exercises more of the external memory (notes, books, websites). These investigations have given rise to new methodological experiences in education.

Finally, we have to take into account that the falling birth rate and economic constraints have increased competition between schools. Many of them have implemented educational changes in which the use of technologies is presented as a differentiating element to compete in a market with scarce students and resources. We must not fall into the trap; technology does not mean higher quality teaching. When parents choose a school, it is prudent for them to research whether the technology that is used or recommended is suitable. They should avoid letting their children become victims of an erroneous educational plan.

In addition, the parents have to determine whether they have enough time and digital literacy to help their children with their digital homework—above all because, in hybrid education, most of the studying is done digitally at home. If the child is young, the time the parents have to dedicate to her is greater than when she already has a certain degree of autonomy. But in all cases, there will always be a need for loving vigilance, attentive help, and closeness.

REMEMBER:

1. Any user can create a blog for free.

2. An imprudent decision caused by a lack of information or an excess of information relegates the success of our decisions to pure chance.

3. No one can guarantee that the information published on the Internet is true.

4. If we find ourselves with too much information and too little time to analyze it, we can feel intellectual anxiety caused by information overload: something known as *infoxication.*

5. Our children should acquire specific digital competencies in order to be part of the information society.

9

MOUNTING THE DEFENSE

IT IS IRRESPONSIBLE NOT TO HAVE a content-filtering system. But it is also irresponsible to install the system and then totally forget about it. This strong statement demands a detailed explanation, which we shall give in this chapter.

WHAT IS A CONTENT FILTER?

A content-filtering system, or simply a content filter, is a program that creates a selective barrier between the user and the information stored on the Internet. The filter analyzes the available navigation information and, taking into account the guidelines defined by the filter administrator (at home, the parents), it allows or blocks access to the information the user requests.

> Filters allow us to analyze, monitor, and prohibit access to certain types of information or certain digital services.

There are many types of filters. The most common one is a Web-page filter. However, there are also other filters, such as connection filters, which block P2P connections, or the filters that block files infected with malware—also known as antivirus programs.

Most companies that manufacture antivirus programs have more complete products that create a single defense against various threats such as spam, phishing, info leaks, viruses, questionable P2P connections, and inappropriate content.

We might think the most important filter in a minor's computer is the Web page filter. That may be true, but not necessarily, at least from the security standpoint. A Web page filter can keep a minor from reaching some inappropriate pages, but if his computer does not have antivirus protection—or if the software is outdated—he runs the risk of a virus or spyware being installed on his computer. If it is not detected by his outdated antivirus, it can look for photographs on his hard drive and send them to the Internet, making them public. This is quite serious when a minor is involved. The malware can also activate the computer's video camera to take a direct image of the person using the computer. We should not become paranoid, but we have to remember that a computer defense system must be organized in depth. The security of our computers and the protection of those who use them is measured by the strength of the weakest link in the security chain. Therefore, it's useless to make an enormous effort to filter content if we simultaneously neglect other security aspects that allow unsuspected intruders to sneak in.

ARE WEB PAGE FILTERING SYSTEMS EFFECTIVE?

Yes, but not enough. That is, they remove some of the danger, but they do not completely get rid of it. We will understand this better if we get an idea of how these filters work.

A Web page is made up of a set of graphic and multimedia elements: text, images, videos, and audios that display and relate to each other in keeping with the Web page's construction format, which is called HTML (HyperText Markup Language). The page also includes information not displayed by the Internet search engine, but still processed by it (the website's metadata): information such as the title, author, structure and format of the images, the code language, various other information used by the search engine, and so on. This metadata controls what is displayed and how it is displayed. Among this metadata, the creator of the page can subjectively classify the page according to its content. For example, if it is a page for adults, the navigator that downloads that page to the computer will show or not show it to the user depending on how the filtering program has been configured *and* on the metadata that the creator of the page has included. So, even the best filter is dependent on how the page creator has classified the page.

> So far things are going well, but no one, before the page is displayed on the computer, tablet, or smart phone, can guarantee that the creator of the Web page has classified his page or has done so correctly? Classification occurs only by the good will of the page creator and in fact, very few Web pages on the Internet follow a classification protocol. Therefore, if you trust the basic filter of the Internet navigator, you will only be able to filter the pages that are classified correctly; the rest will still get through. This is not the best system, or at least it is not the one that protects us most.

A second filtering method consists in doing a *lexicographic analysis* of the page content. If terms appear that we consider unsuitable, the page will not display. This method is more effective than the first one, but it is only applicable to texts, not to images, so any photo or video would be able to get through the filter. In addition, this system produces many *false positives*; that is, it blocks pages that may have an inappropriate word here or there but that should be accessible. For example, let's suppose our content-filtering system does not let pages through that contain the word *rape*. In this case, a page that includes the phrase "the rape of nature" would be blocked by the filter, thus creating a false positive.

To diminish the false positives, filters evaluate the text and assign it a score. Each prohibited word adds points to the page, and that score can be weighted in relation to the semantic or thematic context in which it appears. If the whole page is evaluated and crosses a predetermined threshold, it is blocked; if not, it is transferred to the navigator so it can be displayed.

This filtering system is more generalized and produces fewer false positives, but it can also let some false negatives through, allowing pages with seriously inappropriate content to display. In addition, it is still a method that evaluates *textual information*, not *graphic content*.

A third method consists in having an expert agent evaluate the information contained in a page, text, or images and give it a more or less objective *classification by categories*. Each evaluated and classified page becomes part of a category index. The filters that use this method consult these indices before displaying the pages to the users, who preselected which pages they will accept and which they will reject. Some examples of categories might be sports, news, technology, violence, pornography, or weapons. This method is more effective than the previous ones, since the evaluation also considers the graphic elements on the page. However, it requires that all the pages a user will visit have been previously registered in the correct category index.

There are companies dedicated to creating indices of classified pages, which they later commercialize. This is a very specific and particular method of content creation. However, with this method we are defenseless before hidden pages, which cannot be indexed in any category. This is the case of pages on the deep Internet, which, as we saw, contain much more information than the public Web.

Finally, we have to consider the filtering systems integrated in the Internet search engines. A search engine must recognize all the pages within its reach and create some indices in keeping with the values of the search patterns. This makes them ideal services for filtering pages. Website creators can freely declare that the contents of their pages are for adults; or the search engine itself, using contextual or lexicographical analysis, can classify the pages, images, and videos.

When the navigator accesses the search portal, it will display more or fewer pages depending on the restrictions in the configuration. Normally the search portals offer gently filtered content by default, but we can configure our interaction with the search portal (i.e., we can demand identification of user in the portal) to make the filter very restrictive (low threshold) so that it prevents access to suspicious pages. This system is very interesting. However, it only works if we access the information through search engines. It does not work if we access the page directly without using the search portal.

There are other methods, some of them quite complex, that use artificial intelligence systems to reduce the false negatives and false positives. Content filtering apps today use all these methods together, which makes them more effective, but they are never totally effective. This leads us once again to our golden rule:

> Users can experience the security of a barrier such as a content filter, but what is most important is to have enough maturity to freely and responsibly reject access to pages they should not see. In this way, the filter is just an aid that helps us avoid unpleasant surprises. In any case, a filter acts as a digital condom: It reduces certain risks but does not completely inhibit them.

PARENTAL CONTROL SYSTEMS AND CHILDREN'S BROWSERS

There are apps that can be installed on a child's computer that monitor Web browsing sessions or the environment in which apps are executed, and allow or prevent the minor from performing certain tasks or visiting certain sites. In general, parental control acts in conjunction with a content filtering system. If the minor's age requires it, security can be enhanced with the installation of a children's browser.

When a child tries to access content that is expressly forbidden, it registers the access, and the system either lets him access it or not depending on what his parents have specified. Some parental control apps inform the parent in real time that there is an incident, requesting an explicit permission to grant access. Microsoft Windows, from version 7 onward, incorporates a basic parental control that is easy to set up, and this basic control system can be strengthened by various security suites, which include similar, but more powerful, tools.

A complementary security measure to protecting children is to use children's browsers that are expressly designed for them. Parents can configure them to decide how they will perform and what filter level they will use.

These browsers usually have a very colorful design and offer a very intuitive user experience. They can include children's content, such as educational games or apps, and they use search engines with filtering systems made specifically for children. They protect the computers so children cannot erase important files, and they block access to certain applications installed on the computer. They also can limit the browser's use time. Not all children's browsers offer all of these functions, but the above list gives an idea of what parents can expect when they choose one.

THE FILTER: BARRIER OR CHALLENGE?

Without a doubt, the filter is a barrier, but is it alone always effective? Think about it: What kind of an attitude will many, perhaps most, adolescents have when they find that a filter blocks a website during their browsing session? Many will just turn to other sites that are permitted, but this will not always be the case. If the adolescent is really interested, he will keep trying until he reaches the site or something similar. And one thing is sure: If he puts forth the effort, he will get it. In extreme cases, particularly with computer-savvy minors or in school environments where social status is everything, the filter barrier can become a challenge, since it is an obstacle set in place by someone with authority, which some adolescents view as something to be overcome.

If a student with one of these characteristics finds a hole in the security system that allows him to circumvent the content filter, all the students will know it in a few days—but the teachers will not. The student or group of students who made the discovery will acquire mythical digital prestige, and the other students will admire them and try to imitate them by reaching new achievements.

The worst thing a teacher can do in one of these situations is promote confrontation between the one who set the barrier and the one who fought to overcome it. The best approach is to have an honest conversation to explain the reasons those barriers are in place, and to help the student see that his actions may not only harm others, but may also harm him. In any case, we should not stop setting up the barriers we deem prudent. Failing to do so would be a serious lack of responsibility.

We can also apply these indications to the home front, although normally in this smaller circle the group dynamic is missing and there is usually more privacy in the attempts. This actually increases the exposure to certain types of addiction,[1] although they are less serious in most cases.

> Something to think about: What is the point of installing a content filtering system with a good antivirus at home or at school if our child's cell phone has unlimited access to the Internet?

WHERE TO SITUATE THE FILTERING SYSTEM

This question is very important because, depending on the characteristics of the computer installation, we will have to

---

1. It is said that the leading addiction, at least in the United Kingdom, is coffee, followed by chocolate and then access to Facebook. See *http://www. telegraph.co.uk/news/health/news/4578542/Facebook-coffee-and-chocolate-most-common-British-addictions.html*.

decide on one direction or another. In addition, each system has its advantages and drawbacks.

1. *Installing the filter inside the computer that is used for browsing.* In this case, the filter is a program that is installed on the browsing device, designed to intercept the browser's Internet requests, proceed to their immediate analysis, and make pre-established decisions to block or allow access. With this system, only the computer is protected, but on the other hand, it will always be protected no matter what Internet connection is used. That is, if it is a laptop computer and the child is working at home, at school, or at the library, that computer will be protected, since all content will go through the filter. This system demands a filtering program for every device that accesses the Internet: laptop, cell phone, tablet, and so on.

2. *Installing the filter in the Internet access itself.* In this case, the filtering system is usually purchased from and installed by the same company that sells us our Internet connection service. This system will only keep our computers secure if we use the protected Internet connection, such as our DSL or cable connection. The advantage is that it covers all devices in the house, and we do not need to install (and then maintain) a new application in every single device. This is especially beneficial with a minor's devices that may have difficulty accepting quality filters (because they require too much storage).

3. *Installing a private and centralized filter.* This is a matter of installing a multiuser filtering system that provides the filtering service to all network users. This is the middle ground between the previous two systems

and is widely used in companies, schools, corporations, and other organizations.

Which of the three filtering systems should you choose? If it is an individual computer—and especially if it is a mobile device used in different locations—it is better to opt for installing a filter directly on the device. If you want to protect all the devices in your home, the best option is to purchase the filter from your Internet provider, and if there are mobile devices, you should also install an individual filter on each of those. By contrast, if the devices to be protected are not your responsibility or you do not have control over them and also have to protect many of them (the typical scenario in a business or school), you may want to go for a centralized private filter.

SECURITY IN ONLINE TRANSACTIONS

One of the most inconvenient aspects of online business is the possibility of fraud in electronic transactions: Internet or mobile banking, online shopping, and so on.

In the first place, online shopping itself is very safe if it's done right. It may even be safer than conventional shopping. So why this fear of fraud? And how do we protect ourselves from transactional attacks?

International standards organizations have created a set of protocols to make communications very safe when sensitive processes, such as electronic commerce, require it. All virtual stores and electronic banking services adhere to these protocols, thus guaranteeing certain aspects of security for those who carry out transactions on them.

However, the guarantee depends on the buyers following the necessary security guidelines. For example, suppose that a shopper visits an online store and finds something to buy. She adds the item to the shopping cart and proceeds to make the payment, indicating her form of payment and inputting her data. Once the item is purchased, the seller must mail the item to the buyer's home, usually through a subcontracted logistics company.

But how does the purchase really happen? It happens formally when the payment is made through the store website, which puts four agents into relationship with each other: the buyer, the seller, the seller's bank that receives the payment, and the bank that provides the buyer's credit card.

These four agents communicate through encrypted connections, so they are protected from third parties. It is important to make sure that the connections are encrypted and that the Web pages involved in the purchase are the ones they claim to be. Pay attention to the digital certificates the browser uses, and get into the habit of clicking on the small padlock that indicates the encrypted connection.

Limited interactions are permitted between the four agents involved in the purchase. For example, the buyer interacts with the seller, and the bank that sends the funds interacts with the bank that receives the funds. The buyer interacts with his own bank, and the seller interacts with his. But the store is absolutely not allowed to connect directly to the buyer's bank. Why? For security reasons. The buyer's bank only needs to know how much to pay and to whom, but it does not need to know the buyer's shopping list. In this way, buyers leave no trace of their purchases and avoid having their bank expose them unnecessarily to personalized advertising.

Finally, we should make sure that the online store where we are shopping meets the norms in force at every moment and in every country concerning online shopping.

For example, the website where the buyer shops should clearly specify the seller's social headquarters so the buyer can verify that the seller truly exists.

HOW TO AVOID PHISHING ATTACKS

Another problem related to online transactions is *phishing*, a social engineering attack that can be avoided with a little effort.

Phishing consists in getting a hapless user to do something specific in order to steal his identity. For example, we receive an email telling us that our online banking password has expired and we have to renew it. The email says it comes from our bank, so we do not suspect its veracity. The email may instruct us to click on a hyperlink in order to update the password. As good, obedient citizens, we click on the link, and the browser automatically pulls up the web page.

If we have our suspicions, we can take a closer look to make sure that the page we are seeing is the same one as our bank. But the carefully-crafted counterfeit page often looks very much like the real one. The bogus page will ask us to identify ourselves as we usually do with our credentials (user name and password) and then it will ask for a new password, which we dutifully supply. We will leave the browsing session satisfied because we successfully changed our old password before it expired. Instead, we have fallen into the trap. The web page looked like our bank's web page, but in fact it was not. We didn't notice that, instead of showing the web page of www.mybank.com, it showed the page associated with www.my_bank.com—a very similar address but with a single added underscore. Because we have to supplied the attacker with our user name and our password (the old one, which is supposedly expired), the phisher will then use that information to present himself to our real bank with our real credentials. He now has free rein to do whatever he wants in our account, such as empty it out. The request for a new password was just a ruse to make us feel we have taken care of something that needed to be done, and we will not discover the fraud until the bank sends us a notification that we are in the red. Great, isn't it?

To protect ourselves from this and to encrypt communications, safe websites use electronic documents called digital certificates, which identify the website in an unequivocal way. These certificates are issued by organizations that have the trust of both the banks and their customers. We know we are using a safe connection that has a trustworthy digital certificate because the URL[2] starts with "https" instead of just "http."

In this case, the navigator lets the user know if the bank website's certificate is authentic or not. Some navigators mark the URL in red, while others show a padlock with the security information. The user should always check this information if he wants to be certain of his access, and he should also make sure the address to which he is connecting is identical (not similar, but identical) to the one that is certified as authentic on his digital certificate. With these measures, our electronic transactions will be at least as safe as the ones we do by non-electronic means.

In short, these are the steps you should take to avoid these kinds of fraud:

---

2. The Uniform Resource Locator (URL) is "a location or address identifying where documents can be found on the Internet." See the Oxford Dictionary online at *http://www.oxforddictionaries.com/us/*, 2016.

1. **Do not blindly accept as valid any message or email** that you receive, even though it appears to be coming from someone you know. Viruses are usually sent via email to other people in our name so that the recipients think it is from us and open the email to follow the instructions we supposedly gave them.

2. **Never open attached files in an email if you do not have any guarantees of its origin,** and even then, only open them with caution. Of course, you should never open a file that comes from the Internet (by email or other media) without first having it scanned by an up-to-date antivirus program.

3. A bank or virtual store will never ask you to supply your credentials (passwords, number of credit cards) by electronic means if it is not on the actual purchase page, and then it will always be under a secure connection. Anything else is always fraud.

4. **Keep your computer virus-free** because the malignant action of some viruses is intercepting Internet requests and replacing the landing pages. The probability of this kind of attack can be greatly reduced if your operating systems and applications are up-to-date, including the antivirus software. Remember, this will be impossible if your software is pirated.

5. Security suites with content filters often include an **anti-phishing** module that can help you avoid unpleasant surprises, because they filter out the pages used to attack you.

6. Any transaction which electronically sends personal, sensitive information must be done on a **secure connection** (https or similar) that uses encrypted communications techniques.

7. In any connection, make sure the Internet navigator is presenting you with a **valid digital certificate** of the website you are on. If it is not valid, the browser will ask you if you still want to continue. If you say yes, what happens next is your responsibility. If you say no, the browser will prevent you from accessing the possibly fake page.

8. **Never write your credentials,** particularly your passwords, on paper or on digital files that you could lose or that others could read or steal from you.

SECURITY AND DEFENSE ON MOBILE DEVICES

Mobile devices (smartphones and tablets) with Internet connections are subject to all of the same guidelines about the Internet, but there are some additional aspects that should be taken into account.

Although mobile devices are meant to be used by people, it often seems that people are the ones being used by their mobile devices. A touch of good manners and temperance would suggest that we should not keep them turned on day and night. If we are working on something that requires our attention, we should ask ourselves whether it might be a good idea to remove the cell phone from our work area in order to avoid constant interruptions.

In the case of minors, we should make sure they are getting enough sleep. It is quite common to get messages from minors in the wee hours of the morning, which shows that being fixated on the cell phone led to the minor staying up too late. A child or adolescent (and also an adult) who has acquired these habits will not do well at school or at his job the next day and will probably also be in a bad mood and irritable.

So, at home, create a schedule for using mobile devices, computer games, computers, or television that is flexible, but also must be followed, even if it is just for the sake of order, health, and good manners.

THE MOBILE DEVICE AS A REWARD FOR A MINOR

Not long ago, I was reading a post by Marta Jiménez Serrano on the blog of *El Confidencial*,[3] in which she included the transcript of a YouTube video on a mother's instructions as she gave her thirteen-year-old son a cell phone for Christmas. I asked Marta's permission to reprint the transcription here, because it is very eloquent:

> "What kid today, having reached a certain age, has not begged and pleaded for a mobile phone?"
>
> When we look back at parents' worries about buying their children those first Nokia phones, which could barely send text messages and make or receive calls, they almost seem silly. Now, when we buy a child a mobile phone, we are giving him a window that grants him access to the entire world of the Internet.
>
> Janell Hoffman, the mother of Greg Hoffman, knows it very well. The child, thirteen years old, had been sighing for a mobile phone for a year. He begged, implored, and pleaded, but he got nothing...until the most recent Christmas, when he got his much-desired iPhone.
>
> However, the device came with a contract written by his mother:

---

3. *El Confidencial* is a Spanish newspaper.

Dear Gregory,

Merry Christmas! You are now the proud owner of an iPhone. . . . You are a good and responsible thirteen-year-old boy and you deserve this gift. But with the acceptance of this present come rules and regulations. Please read through the following contract. I hope that you understand it is my job to raise you into a well-rounded, healthy young man who can function in the world and coexist with technology, not be ruled by it. Failure to comply with the following list will result in termination of your iPhone ownership.

I love you madly and look forward to sharing several million text messages with you in the days to come.

1. *It is my phone. I bought it. I pay for it. I am loaning it to you. Aren't I the greatest?*

2. *I will always know the password.*

3. *If it rings, answer it. It is a phone. Say hello; use your manners. Do not ever ignore a phone call if the screen reads "Mom" or "Dad." Not ever.*

4. *Hand the phone to one of your parents promptly at 7:30 pm every school night and every weekend night at 9:00 pm. It will be shut off for the night and turned on again at 7:30 am. If you would not make a call to someone's landline because their parents might answer first, then do not call or text. Listen to those instincts and respect other families the way we would like to be respected.*

5. *It does not go to school with you. Have a conversation in person with the people you text. It's a*

life skill. *Half days, field trips, and after-school activities will require special consideration.

6. If it falls into the toilet, smashes on the ground, or vanishes into thin air, you are responsible for the replacement costs or repairs. Mow a lawn, babysit, stash some birthday money. It will happen, so you should be prepared.

7. Do not use this technology to lie, fool, or deceive another human being. Do not involve yourself in conversations that are hurtful to others. Be a good friend first or stay the hell out of the crossfire.

8. Do not text, email, or say anything through this device you would not say in person.

9. Do not text, email, or say anything to someone that you would not say out loud with their parents in the room. Censor yourself.

10. No porn. Search the Web for information you would openly share with me. If you have a question about anything, ask a person—preferably me or your father.

11. Turn it off, silence it, put it away in public. Especially in a restaurant, at the movies, or while speaking with another human being. You are not a rude person; do not allow the iPhone to change that.

12. Do not send or receive pictures of your private parts or anyone else's private parts. Don't laugh. Someday you will be tempted to do this despite your high intelligence. It is risky and could ruin your teenage/college/adult life. It is always a bad idea. Cyberspace is vast and more powerful than

you. And it is hard to make anything of this magnitude disappear—including a bad reputation.

13. *Don't take a zillion pictures and videos. There is no need to document everything. Live your experiences. They will be stored in your memory for eternity.*

14. *Leave your phone home sometimes and feel safe and secure in that decision. It is not alive or an extension of you. Learn to live without it. Be bigger and more powerful than FOMO (fear of missing out).*

15. *Download music that is new or classic or different than the millions of your peers that listen to the same exact stuff. Your generation has access to music like never before in history. Take advantage of that gift. Expand your horizons.*

16. *Play a game with words or puzzles or brain teasers every now and then.*

17. *Keep your eyes up. See the world happening around you. Stare out a window. Listen to the birds. Take a walk. Talk to a stranger. Wonder without googling.*

18. *You will mess up. I will take away your phone. We will sit down and talk about it. We will start over again. You and I, we are always learning. I am on your team. We are in this together.*

It is my hope that you can agree to these terms. Most of the lessons listed here do not just apply to the iPhone, but to life. You are growing up in a fast and ever-changing world. It is exciting and enticing. Keep it simple every chance you get. Trust your powerful

> *mind and giant heart above any machine. I love you. I hope you enjoy your awesome new iPhone.*
>
> *xoxoxo,*
> *Mom*[4]

No further comment needed.

REMEMBER:

1. A content-filtering system, or just a content filter, is a program that sets up a selective barrier between the user and the information stored on the Internet.

2. Users can enjoy the security of a content filter, but the most important thing is to have enough maturity to freely and responsibly reject access to what you should not see.

3. Browsers designed specifically for children are complementary security measure for kids.

4. *Phishing* consists in getting the user to input information in order to steal his identity.

5. At home, mobile devices, computer games, computers, or the television should have a schedule that is flexible, but that must be followed, even if it is just for the sake of order, health, and good manners.

---

4. Quoted in Janell Burley Hofmann, "To My 13-Year-Old, An iPhone Contract from Your Mom, with Love," 12/28/2012, *http://www.huffingtonpost. com/janell-burley-hofmann/iphone-contract-from-your-mom_b_2372493. html*.

10

CYBER-STALKING

PARENTS AND EDUCATORS HAVE an important role to play in reducing the risks to the children under their care. They have a mission to lead and accompany their children or students when they begin using new technologies. If an adult is unaware of these dangers, the minor will be exposed to risks that could have been avoided. So the adult's formation is even more important than that of the minor.

The two biggest dangers are *cyberbullying* (students stalking other students) and *grooming*, which involves adults stalking minors.

Cyberbullying occurs when minors, usually students, stalk other minors using the Internet, cell phones, smartphones, video games, and so on. Both the stalker and the victim typically are minors of a similar age. Cyberbullying is usually associated with threats, insults, humiliation, or the creation of fake profiles on the social networks that take the place of the potential victim's real identity, associating him or her with offensive content, and tagging people with a clearly offensive intention.

If the stalker is an adult and the stalked person is a minor, and there is an implicit or explicit sexual purpose behind the stalking, then we are talking about grooming. In this kind of stalking, the adult carries out a series of actions intended to gain the minor's trust in order to get sexual favors: He draws close with empathy, deceit, and blackmail to get compromising images of the minor, and in extreme cases, he arranges a personal encounter with the minor.

Experts say that these phenomena occur because minors are jumping into the new technologies without enough education regarding security or without enough helpful information on how to deal with cyber-stalking. Additionally, there is a certain lack of knowledge on the importance of privacy, both one's own and others'. An education in modesty and self-respect could help minors improve their self-defense, because both virtues help protect their privacy.

On the other hand, minors must understand the potentially viral nature of information that is published online. Information on the Internet can go unnoticed or it can unleash a chain reaction (i.e., the content can *go viral*). Writing "John is stupid" on the door of a bathroom stall in a bar is not the same as writing it on someone's social network profile.

Various people are involved in cyber-stalking cases: the stalker, the victim, and the spectators, who can encourage the cyber-stalking or consent to it. When we study one of these cases, we must take into account the action or omission of these agents. We should also think of something fundamental: the sensation of impunity with which stalkers commit their criminal acts, reinforced by the protection of anonymity behind which they hide, and which the Internet fosters.

Some types of stalking that are currently trending are *sexting* and *happy slapping*. *Sexting* consists in recording and sending erotic or pornographic content through mobile devices (normally phones, which are more manageable), something that is increasingly common for young people and adolescents. *Happy slapping* consists in recording fights through cell phones with the intent of publishing them on social networks or content sharing platforms.

In general, minors are more aware of cyber-stalking incidents than their parents, which leads one to think that many parents are unaware of what is going on with their children. It is estimated that parents are aware that their children are being stalked in only half of the cases. Although it is difficult to specify, some statistics say the rate of minors who suffer from stalking alone (not taking into account technical risks, the loss of privacy, or access to inappropriate content, which would be much more) is between 5 and 10 percent. This should make us tremble.

> Parents, think about it: Your child could be living through this situation. Teachers: Some of your students could be suffering bullying in the classroom, and a classmate could be a cyberbully.

In the case of *grooming*, the stalker initiates a phase of friendship during which he makes contact with a minor and gets familiar with some of his or her likes and preferences. His goal is to move into the second phase of the relationship, becoming a confidante or sharer of secrets in order to solidify the relationship of trust. Next the sexual component of the relationship will appear. Thus the grooming trajectory follows the path of contact and approach, virtual sex, cyber-stalking with blackmail and abuse, and possible sexual aggression. Grooming, through contact with an unknown adult, happens much less than cyberbullying, but it is still a significant concern.

HOW TO TELL WHEN A MINOR IS BEING CYBERBULLIED

Experts suggest some signs that indicate a minor is being cyberbullied, or that he himself is a bully. Although these signs are possible symptoms, they are not precise indicators of a crime or an attitude or predisposition to cyberbullying, so we are not trying to raise any unnecessary alarms.

A CYBERBULLY USUALLY HAS THE FOLLOWING CHARACTERISTICS:

- A strong need to dominate others. He likes to use physical strength.
- Low academic performance.
- Impulsiveness and low tolerance for frustration.
- Difficulties accepting and following rules.
- Strong tendency to violent attitudes.
- Little empathy toward the victims of his or others' aggressions.
- His relationships with adults are usually aggressive.
- The protagonist both of proactive aggression (deliberate acts intended to reach an objective) and of reactive aggression (self-defense when provoked).

VICTIMS USUALLY HAVE THE FOLLOWING CHARACTERISTICS:

- *Changes in their habits:* the use of electronic devices or on the Internet, their class attendance, their usual leisure activities, their relationships with adults, their eating habits,

Continued

Continued

> ### VICTIMS USUALLY HAVE THE FOLLOWING CHARACTERISTICS:
>
> dropping the activities that used to be their favorites, ups and downs in their studies or in their grades, lack of capacity for concentration, and changing their groups of friends or acquaintances.
>
> - *Changes in their mood:* mood swings, sadness, apathy, indifference, periods of relaxation and tension, unusual aggressiveness, or extreme reserve in communication.
> - *Changes in their social network:* sudden loss or surge in contacts, lack of self-defense against supposed public or harmless jokes, fear or unwillingness to leave home.
> - *Physical changes or changes in their physical belongings:* changes in their body language, such as slumped shoulders, bowed head, lack of eye contact, unwillingness to appear in public, taking up unique public spaces like corners or protected spaces, specific measures to hide his or her identity when surfing the Internet, signs of sickness or frequent aches or pains, loss or deterioration of physical belongings, unexplained physical wounds.
> - *Bodily changes:* rapid increase or loss of weight as a consequence of changed eating habits, frequent dizzy spells with uncommon symptoms, headaches or stomach aches that do not cause a lack of sleep but hamper ordinary daily activities, frequent diarrhea that is not accompanied by vomiting or fever.

HOW TO TREAT THE STALKED MINOR

If we suspect that a minor is being stalked in some way, the issue should be faced through communication and the establishment of trust between the adults and the minor in their care. The approach should be primarily *emotional*. If a minor is really being bullied, she is living through a situation of confusion and shame that she does not know how to deal with: She will probably try to hide the real situation. The first thing an adult must do is make sure the minor does not feel guilty about what she thinks is happening to her.

> The adult should convince the bullied minor that he can speak freely and in confidence, that he totally understands his situation, that he is ready to help him, and that he has the parents' permission to undertake the steps they will take together.

So, the way forward is to *foster communication, avoid blame,* and *show trust.* If necessary, once the issue has been resolved, set up educational measures to avoid any possibly imprudent situations that may have led to stalking. But this step should not be taken until a relationship of deep trust has been established, and until the problem has been solved or is on its way toward being resolved.

It is ineffective to let time pass, avoid action, let oneself be carried away by fear, seek confrontation online, or be indifferent. If the matter is serious, it will be necessary to document the case and report the offense to proper authority. We will have to look for support and information or, if need be, turn to the help of specialists who can diagnose and treat the issues caused by the stalking.

PREVENTION

Prevention is the primary mission of parents and educators. It begins with good communication within the family. We cannot build this kind of communication as a last resort; it has to be done early and well, in an atmosphere of deep love and affection. We must exercise sensitivity and we should always express respect for the victim and his rights.

> Minors should be educated in ethical values in keeping with their age and guided to develop cause-and-effect thinking. That is, they should be taught that their actions have consequences for which they will be responsible, and that their actions can hurt themselves or others.

Cooperation between the school and the family is very important to resolve stalking problems effectively, above all because victims tend to want to hide it from public view. This leads to burying the problem rather than solving it, and the stalker ends up enjoying impunity, which will then lead him to continue offending. At the same time, it will prevent the victim from getting the treatment he or she needs to correct the imbalance caused by the stalking.

Educators have a degree of civil responsibility as legal guardians during school hours. The school has the authority to enact disciplinary measures against any cyberbullying that affects the school community, taking into account that the teacher is a public authority and enjoys the presumption of truth. A school should have guidelines for action that at least guarantee a channel of communication to report suspicions of stalking. Those in charge should analyze this report as quickly as possible.

> In any case, the victim should never answer a provocation of cyber-stalking, but should report the crime to the competent authorities. If the stalking takes

place in a school, then the school authorities should inform the parents so that they can take the appropriate action in conjunction with the school.

The case of a minor who is a bully is also very delicate. The parents should question their son or daughter to find out if he or she is a bully or is part of a group engaging in bullying. Parents can use news reports about cyberbullying in order to ask questions like, "Could you ever be an aggressor? Could you ever be a victim? Or could you ever be a coward who takes the bully's side instead of the victim's side?" Any question presented to the bullying minor or the victim should be posed in a very open-ended way so the minor has the chance to express everything that is happening without holding back.

REMEMBER:

1. Cyber-stalking and cyberbullying occur because minors are jumping into the new technologies without enough support regarding security or helpful information.
2. Become familiar with the characteristics of someone who is being cyberbullied.
3. When treating a minor who is being stalked, adults should strive to *foster communication, avoid blame,* and *show trust.*
4. Prevention is the primary mission of parents and educators when it comes to the danger of new technologies.
5. Parents can use news reports of cyberbullying to engage their children in conversation, making sure to ask open-ended questions.

11

---·---

GUIDELINES FOR TECHNOLOGICAL EDUCATION

JUST AS WE TEACH YOUNG CHILDREN how to use a spoon or fork, not go anywhere with strangers, or look both ways before crossing the street, we also should teach them how to use new technologies. The guidelines for a minor's technological education should take into account the minor's security, considering all the psycho-developmental aspects in keeping with his or her age or circumstances.

GUIDELINES FOR PARENTS

Experts recommend starting technological education as early as possible. The idea is for minors to experience technology as something natural from the very start. This should not prevent parents from taking the necessary precautions, because any educational process should be guided. The guidelines should be adapted to the child's age and capacity, not just regarding the type of content, but also the type of activity.

We cannot teach a four-year-old child how to use email or set up a social network profile, but we can train four-year-olds to use an educational online video game in which they color, read their first letters, identify animals, and so on. These activities will help young children to acquire dexterity with the mouse or touch screen. Parents should choose what they think is best for their child at each stage, perhaps in cooperative communication with their child's teachers, who can also guide the child in making these decisions.

> Thus, from a young age we will use technology with our children, helping them to understand that this is not unusual activity or something isolated from the rest of life. In this way, their educational process will be guided and harmonious, integrated into the rest of their activities. The child will not think of technology as a reward, which could create obsessive or compulsive habits. If the child has a technological problem in the future, he or she will handle it with his parents or teacher in the same way that he or she would handle something in a non-technological area.

The work of the family in educating a child is based on initiation, access, follow-up, accompanying, and guidance in the use and consumption of new technologies, which are agreed upon in the family circle. We have to explain in clear language, with arguments that are suited to the minor's age and circumstances, how to behave. It is not about trying to force our children to respect our norms as it is about educating them so they value what those norms represent, and are able to decide for themselves (particularly as they become adolescents), although we possibly run the risk that they will occasionally make mistakes. Part of the educational process consists in learning to correct their mistakes and draw positive lessons from them.

The MenoresOSI organization[1] recommends the following fundamental aspects that parents should take into account:

- Parents should *know their children's online friends, the apps they use, and their interests*, sharing their browsing activity with them. They should show their children in an age-appropriate way the dangers they will find in real life. With common sense, they should help minors understand that whatever would be wrong in their physical surroundings is also wrong in online browsing and relationships.

- *Speak to minors about the dangers* that might lie in wait for them. For example, they may confuse chatting with supposed friends who turn out not to be friends. Parents also should pay special attention to sexual content.

- *Pay attention to the games, photographs, or videos* that children receive, exchange, or copy, because these can be damaging for their education and development. In this sense, we have to explain to them that not all of them are fun and some are even dangerous, violent, pornographic, and harmful. We should emphasize why they should not allow themselves to be convinced by the supposed economic advantages of illegal copies of games, software, movies, and music, explaining the disadvantages and dangers they involve, such as computer viruses.

- *Share information with the children about computer news* and encourage adolescents who show interest in computers to share their knowledge with their parents, siblings, relatives, and friends. This activity will provide insight into their personal interests.

---

1. See *https://menores.osi.es*.

Interaction with children should be in the form of dialogue so parents can get the information they need to educate and protect their children. This information can be obtained without subjecting the child to the third degree, formulating some questions that MenoresOSI suggests:

- *What do your friends do on the Internet?* With this question, we focus attention on the child's friendships. It is a good way to start and maintain a neutral and generic chat. It is not a good idea to scold or punish a child for his answers, if we want our child to answer sincerely. In addition, in this indirect way, we are also getting to know how our child uses the Internet, since it is very likely that his likes are very similar to those of his friends. If we ask the question in a more direct way ("What do you do on the Internet?"), the child might feel threatened or probed, so his answer will more likely be irrelevant or evasive. Worse, we could end up damaging our bond of communication with our child and begin to lose trust.

- *What are the trendy websites these days?* To be up-to-date, ask your child what is in style and why. In the same way, you can ask her why there are sites that were more popular before but now aren't. That will tell you what kinds of things she looks for on the Internet and what she enjoys.

- *Do you want me to show you the pages I like on the Internet?* Afterward you can move on to the suggestion "Show me which are your favorite pages." In this way you will get to know what your child really does on the Internet. Use the opportunity to share knowledge, experience, and concerns with your child. You can also use this moment to help him configure his accounts correctly and protect his privacy.

- *Have you ever seen anything strange or anything that made you feel uncomfortable online?* This question is meant to create an opening to talk about some websites your child should not visit because they host content that is unsuitable for her age. The goal is to make sure she knows that she can count on you if she mistakenly ends up at a website with these characteristics, and that she will not be punished for it. Bad experiences on the Internet are almost inevitable. We need to make sure we have our children's trust so that, if there are problems, they will come to us for help and protection.

- *Ask him about cyber-stalking.* Your child may not know it by the terms cyberbullying or grooming, but he almost certainly knows what it is. Try talking to him about stories that you heard in the media about disagreeable emails, "compromising" photographs, blackmail, or personal information that was shared using the social networks, blogs, or email to see how your child reacts to these stories. Make sure that he knows how to act if he is ever faced with these situations: Do not respond to the stalker's jokes or insults; do not participate in spreading the mockery or bullying of another child; do not contact strangers on the Internet; and so on.

- *Ask your children about the emails they get.* If on some occasion you receive a phishing email or a message with some attached file that carries a virus, it would be good to ask your child—and at the same time, guide her—on what to do with that email. Ask her if she thinks it could be a virus; ask her if she thinks you should scan it with the anti-virus program to see if it is infected. In this way, you are teaching her how to detect threats.

- *Ask your child if he respects privacy.* It is also important to ask your child if he knows how to configure the privacy settings on the social network he uses. You can look at the various options and do it together. This way, you will learn from each other about how to configure the privacy settings, while also being aware of its importance.

SOME USEFUL ADVICE FOR PARENTS

As general guidelines, parents should bear in mind the following tips INTECO offers in its security guide:[2]

In general

1. Parents need to know enough about computers to be able to teach their children to use them from the start.
2. Foster dialogue about browsing habits and their risks.
3. Agree to some rules for use that will be clear to the whole family.
4. Use protection systems based on content filters, anti-virus protection, firewalls, and the like.
5. Put computers with an Internet connection in common living areas to make it easier to supervise and monitor in case of problems.
6. Teach children about privacy and how to protect it; educate them in modesty and respect for themselves and others.

Children ages 4 to 12

1. Guide them in the use of the computer.
2. Know the user names and the services that they use, and help them choose passwords that are strong enough to prevent anyone from stealing their identity.

---

2. *Guide to Security and Privacy of Geolocation Tools*, INTECO, March 2011.

3. Teach them not to download anything without an adult's permission.

Children ages 13 to 18

1. We have to bear in mind that most adolescents want more autonomy regarding their own thoughts, decisions, and activities, and they might perceive questions to be an intrusion of their privacy.
2. Since kids in this age range are already using email, teach them to distinguish between spam and legitimate mail. They should not read anything that comes from an unknown sender.
3. Be attentive to whether they have contacted a stranger.
4. Teach them to act responsibly and respectfully. If they would not do something in real life, they should not do it on the Internet, hiding behind the anonymity that the Web offers.
5. Make sure they check with you before making any electronic transactions.

FOR READERS WHO ARE KIDS

If you, dear reader, are a minor, read attentively the following guidelines that are offered to you.[3] Or, if you are a father, mother, or tutor, I suggest that you read this short text and then share it with the minors in your care.

It is possible that you may have heard stories about abuses of children on the Internet, whether through unwanted proposals from adults or through access to sexual or violent

---

3. See *http://www.segu-kids.org*.

content. In any case, you have to protect yourself on the Internet from any stranger, just as you would in real life. This is a series of guidelines that you should take into account in order to use the Internet wisely.

General advice about the Internet

1. Do not register your personal information on chats, blogs, or unprotected social networks so this information will not be available to people with bad intentions.

2. Do not share your personal information or your family's information (names, address, phone numbers) on the Internet, and do not give your user name and password to anyone.

3. Do not meet with people you've met online without your parents' permission. There are people who lie about their age or their intentions, and they can hurt you.

4. Do not answer messages that make you feel uncomfortable or ashamed. Tell your parents everything if this happens to you.

5. If anyone makes you feel uncomfortable in a conversation, immediately end the conversation and tell your parents.

6. Record conversations you have on chat with other people so you can show it to someone if necessary.

7. Do not send photos of yourself or your family to contacts you do not know, and never publish them on the Internet without your family's knowledge.

8. Ignore all spam messages, and do not open files from people you don't know; they might contain something harmful. It is possible that someone could use these means to figure out your chat password or your email

password in order to steal your data and infect your computer with a virus.

9. Do not use your webcam to chat, since someone could take pictures of you and then use them against you or someone in your family. When it is not being used, the webcam should be covered up by an opaque object that prevents it from getting any images.

10. Do not identify yourself with a nickname or digital name that reveals your birthdate or age or any other private data. For example: Anna_05 could reveal that you were born in 2005 or john_13 could mean that you are a thirteen-year-old boy.

11. Use safe passwords and do not give them out to anyone, because anyone who has your password could pass himself off as you. Only you and your parents should know your passwords.

12. On social networks, do not accept strangers as contacts or friends, and make your profile private so that only your friends and acquaintances can see it.

13. Do not share personal information that could be used to identify you, such as names, addresses, or phone numbers.

14. Do not respond to obscene, aggressive, or sexual harassment messages. If you get such a message, immediately tell your parents.

15. Give your information only to people you know personally, and even then, only when it is necessary.

16. Ask your parents or teachers any questions that you might have about how to use any Internet service.

17. Remember that the difference between good and bad is the same on the Internet as it is in real life.

18. Use parental controls or a content-filtering application to manage sites you access and their content. In this way, you are protecting yourself.

19. Respect others' property. Downloading or making illegal copies of another's work (music, video games, and other programs) can be considered an act of plagiarism, theft, or piracy, and it can pose a legal problem for your family.

20. Remember that what you read, hear, or see on the Internet can be false.

Specific guidelines about social networks

1. Organize your contacts by groups. When you publish something, do it prudently, selecting the groups of contacts you want to have access to your information. For example, if you post a personal photo, perhaps it is not a good idea for people outside your family to see it.

2. Do not post photos of other persons, images, or cartoons on your profile.

3. Do not set up a personal meeting with someone on the Internet, because you can attract people with bad intentions. It is not a good idea to look for people on the Internet in order to meet them later in real life. But if you do, make sure you meet in a public place with plenty of people around so you can get help if something goes wrong.

4. When you express an opinion on the Internet, take into account that many people will see what you publish.

5. Social networks have made it very easy to accept an invitation to join a group. Be careful about which invitations you accept.

6. Do not tolerate criminal or nasty behavior and do not verbally abuse other people online.

7. Do not post content that is pornographic or in poor taste, or is considered advertising or spam.

Specific guidelines for cyberstalking

1. Avoiding cyberbullying or cyber-stalking requires knowing what to do if you become a victim. If you are a victim of any kind of stalking through the Internet, it is important for you to realize that you are not alone and that you can always do something to prevent it.

2. Tell your parents or teachers so that they can make a decision about what to do and report it as needed.

3. Bear in mind that most websites where videos, texts, or photographs are published have terms of use that expressly prohibit the reproduction of unlawful material or material that is aggressive or offensive toward someone else. If you are targeted in a video, photo, or text on a website, report it to the website administrator so that the content is deleted.

4. If you receive messages you do not like or those that make you feel bad in any way, remember that you can block that person so you do not receive anything else from them.

5. Do not respond to a stalker, because that will not solve the problem. Have the courage to run away.

6. Do not establish relationships with strangers without checking their identity. When in doubt, reject the contact.

7. Keep your personal information personal. Do not send sensitive information to strangers.

8. Do not publish anyone else's personal information or any data that does not belong to you.

9. Do not be complicit or cooperate in the publication of any kind of content that could damage someone else.

10. Remember that almost nothing can be kept private on the Internet. What one person can see, others can see.

If you are a victim of cyberbullying or of any kind of cyber-stalking, remember the SBT rule: Stop, Block, and Tell. *Stop* means do not do anything and take five minutes to think. *Block* the media or limit communications. And *tell* an adult you trust and get his or her help.

REMEMBER:

1. When educating kids in the use of the new technologies, parents should introduce them to it, help them gain responsible access, keep track of what they do, and guide them through it.

2. Interaction with kids should be done through dialogue, so the parents can get the information they need to educate and protect them.

3. Parents should be trained in using the computer and should know its benefits and risks so they can teach and protect their kids.

EPILOGUE
It's Worth It

AFTER READING THIS BOOK, you might think that technology consists of more risks than benefits and you might be tempted to conclude that the use of the Internet entails too many prohibitions: "Don't say this; don't do that; don't touch that." But that's not the whole picture. It is clear that there are risks, but so does ordinary life, whether we leave the house every day or stay inside.

Effectively exploiting the possibilities of the Internet requires knowing the medium, especially if we want to do things well. As in other areas, doing it well requires a learning process. It is not enough to want it—we have to do it. And for that, we have to know how.

So if we adopt a sensible attitude toward the Internet, we will not just focus on the risks and self-defense; we will focus most of our attention on how to exploit all of its possibilities for our own benefit and for the benefit of others, knowing that this new media opens up many new doors.

The Internet is a gigantic worldwide speaker that amplifies everything that is published. If we manage or spread erroneous or harmful information, we will do great damage. But if we work with quality information, we can also do immense good. Aren't we going to make the most of this possibility to do good?

For example, we can spread healthy, well-founded, logically argued ideas about our philosophy of life, presenting a transcendent view of human events and showing our agreement or disagreement with the ideas proposed by others.

There are people who blog regularly on a specific topic and who gradually become experts on it and become a point of reference in that professional, social, moral, or entertainment field. You can also participate actively on social networks to promote ethical viewpoints or defend social causes to which you feel committed. You can create campaigns to help with specific needs. And you can improve your professional formation. The possibilities are endless.

You also can use the Internet to improve your relationships with others and strengthen the bonds between people. In the end, a person's influence is measured by the quality of the relationships he or she freely develops. Thus, the freedom to commit ourselves enriches us more than anything else. For example, through social networks, electronic messaging, or video conferencing, we can be present at any time and in any part of the world to accompany, congratulate, help, or show our support to almost anyone and in almost any situation. Physical distance is no longer a significant obstacle in the relationships that unite us to other people.